Dare to dream
+ to do!

Praise for *Daring Visionaries*

"Ray Smilor's book takes you inside the hearts and minds of entrepreneurs—painting a vivid picture of what it takes to be a successful entrepreneur. A compelling and inspiring book on both the risks and rewards of entrepreneurship."
—Mario Morino, Chairman, Morino Institute

"*Daring Visionaries* is an honest, forthcoming and motivational portrayal of the reality entrepreneurs face in today's world. It's a provocative piece with an unparalleled perspective on the subject of entrepreneurs and the entrepreneurial process."
—Dr. J. Robert Beyster, Chairman and CEO,
Science Applications International Corporation

"Ray Smilor brings to the exploration of entrepreneurship a unique insight which combines both practical knowledge and the ability to integrate individual stories into a lively and engaging learning experience."
—Dr. Sharon Hadary, Executive Director,
National Foundation for Women Business Owners

"Dr. Ray Smilor really knows entrepreneurs, and you will too when you read—when you experience—*Daring Visionaries*."
—Dr. Robert Lawrence Kuhn, President,
The Geneva Companies; Host, *Closer to Truth* Public Television Series

"*Daring Visionaries* clearly demonstrates how the passion of entrepreneurs can turn apparent defeat into victory and dreams into realities. It shows, with insight and humor, what's really important in starting and growing a company."
—Jim McCann, Chairman, CEO, 1-800-FLOWERS

"Ray Smilor peels away the veneer and hits us right between the eyes with the naked truth about the rough and tumble world of entrepreneurship. Sit up and take notes: *Daring Visionaries* will be of help to you no matter how you earn your living."
—Dennis P. Kimbro, Author,
Think and Grow Rich: A Black Choice

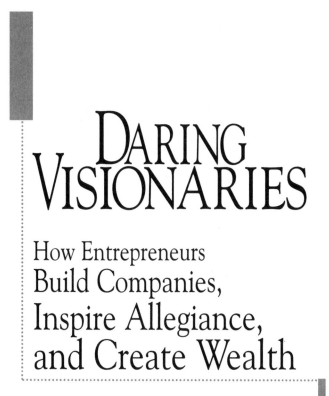

DARING VISIONARIES

How Entrepreneurs Build Companies, Inspire Allegiance, and Create Wealth

RAY SMILOR

ADAMS MEDIA CORPORATION
Avon, Massachusetts

To my parents
Maureen and Wes Smilor
In memoriam

Published by
Adams Media Corporation
57 Littlefield Street, Avon, MA 02322. U.S.A.
www.adamsmedia.com

ISBN: 1-58062-476-6

Printed in Canada.

J I H G F E D C B

Library of Congress Cataloging-in-Publication Data
Smilor, Raymond W.
Daring visionaries : how entrepreneurs build companies, inspire
allegiance, and create wealth / Raymond W. Smilor.
p.   cm.
ISBN 1-58062-476-6
1. Entrepreneurship. 2. Success in business. 3. Entrepreneurship–Case studies.
4. Success in business–Case studies. I. Title.
HB615 .S64   2001
658.4'21--dc21   2001022401

Table of Contents

Section III: Skills of Entrepreneurs

Section IV: Experience of Entrepreneurship

Section V: Managing the Dark Side

Section VI: Social Impact of Entrepreneurship

Foreword

Evangelists
and Revolutionaries

This book is about evangelists and revolutionaries—those daring souls who envision a better world, blaze new trails in business, and upset the status quo.

I know a few things about evangelists and revolutionaries. I think I've been both, worked with both, and funded both. I've come to the conclusion that all successful entrepreneurs have the elements of both within them.

As evangelists, entrepreneurs believe so deeply in what they are about that they bring a crusading zeal to turning their visions into realities. They have to. So many entrepreneurs are told that they're crazy, that their ideas will never work, that what they propose just can't be done. And yet, time and again, they seem to do the impossible. Their ability to overcome obstacles, to persist in the face of adversity, and to win converts to their causes comes from the soul of the entrepreneur that Ray Smilor so eloquently describes.

I first learned about evangelism when I was at Apple Computer, where I held the title of software evangelist. I learned that with fervor, guts, and smarts, an entrepreneur could make the people who worked with him, the financiers who funded him, and even his customers as passionate about his cause as he was. How he goes about doing this is reflected in the secrets and skills of entrepreneurs that Ray delineates.

As revolutionaries, entrepreneurs defy conventional wisdom, push the boundaries of technological know-how, and challenge the status quo. This is part of their great contribution to economic growth and vitality. By constantly coming up with innovative products and services, devising better ways of doing things, and even creating new industries, entrepreneurs serve as the catalyst for the economic churn that is so essential to a healthy and vibrant economy.

At Garage.com, we're working to develop a whole new approach to how companies get funded. Using the Internet, we're changing the rules of the game in terms of how entrepreneurs may access capital, and changing the rules of the game is exactly what entrepreneurs work to do. This is what Ray communicates in discussing the experience of the entrepreneur.

I am convinced that the entrepreneur's role is to make the world a better place and to reap some economic rewards for doing so. However, the economic rewards are an outcome of making the world a better place. They are not the reason for becoming an entrepreneur. In this sense, entrepreneurs have both the opportunity and responsibility to make a positive and constructive contribution to the society of which they are a part, just as Ray outlines in discussing the social impact of entrepreneurship. Then, having reaped economic rewards, entrepreneurs have a moral obligation to make the world an even better place by giving back to the community and country that make their success possible.

This compelling book captures the spirit and drama of entrepreneurs. With wit and wisdom, it inspires while it informs. And it challenges anyone who is or who wants to be an entrepreneur to dare to dream and to do.

Guy Kawasaki
CEO
Garage.com

The Faces of Entrepreneurship

When you look in the mirror, do you see the face of an entrepreneur?

Today, statistics show that more people are starting companies than ever before in American history; new and emerging companies are the source of all net new job creation; women are launching companies at faster rates than men; minorities are starting companies in record numbers; more colleges and universities are teaching entrepreneurship to classrooms full of students; communities across the country are creating organizations to support entrepreneurs; and larger, more traditional companies are striving to become more entrepreneurial. As a result, entrepreneurship has become the social and economic phenomenon of our times.

Behind every statistic of entrepreneurship is the face of an entrepreneur. Maybe your face.

The face of entrepreneurship is the face of the start-up-in-the-basement entrepreneur, like Danny O'Neill, the self-proclaimed "bean baron," who has built a thriving gourmet coffee business from the basement of his house.

The face of entrepreneurship is the face of the downsized entrepreneur, like Rick Krska, who now employs over 120 people in his business of remanufacturing ink jet and toner cartridges after being laid off at a *Fortune* 500 company.

The face of entrepreneurship is the face of the welfare-to-work entrepreneur, like Phyliss Brockman, who started her own janitorial business to find a better life for herself and her four daughters.

The face of entrepreneurship is the face of the accidental entrepreneur, like Ann-Merelie Morrell, who wound up running a glass manufacturing company after she discovered it was housed inside a building she had purchased.

The face of entrepreneurship is the face of the crisis-driven entrepreneur, like Mary Anne Mattox, who created a natural foods bakery after helping her husband deal with lung cancer through a macrobiotic diet of organic grains and beans.

The face of entrepreneurship is the face of the career-changing entrepreneur, like Kay Hammer, who left an academic position in linguistics to launch a software company.

The face of entrepreneurship is the face of the social entrepreneur, like Bill Strickland, who turned a passion for pottery into a not-for-profit training center for inner city youth and adults.

And the face of entrepreneurship is the face of the take-care-of-the-family entrepreneur, like Ewing Marion Kauffman, who started a pharmaceutical company to provide for his family, and then learned that he could grow it into a multibillion-dollar corporation.

The face of entrepreneurship in our society today includes other faces as well—the faces of elementary school teachers and college professors, the faces of community supporters and business incubator directors, the faces of investors and mentors, the faces of policy makers and regulators—all of whom are part of the entrepreneurial revolution that is now shaping the society and economy of the twenty-first century.

The face of entrepreneurship is my face. And according to national estimates, if you are one of the seven million Americans who are trying to start a business at any given time, then the face of entrepreneurship is your face. Or if you are one of the 50 percent of adult Americans or the 70 percent of high school students who would like to be his or her own boss and control his or her own destiny by starting a business, then the face of entrepreneurship is your face, too.

Acknowledgments

From start to finish in writing this book, I have benefited from the example, encouragement, and support of entrepreneurial people and organizations. They have enriched my experience and improved this manuscript by bringing their own passion, in one way or another, to this venture.

I have had the good fortune to know personally many of the entrepreneurs who are featured here. Their stories, experiences, and lessons learned have informed and inspired me, as I hope they will others.

I got to know Ewing Kauffman before his death in August 1993. I remember my one-on-one's with him and the vision that he provided. The opportunity he gave me to help build the Kauffman Center has been one of the most rewarding personal and professional experiences of my life. The support and commitment of the Center have been invaluable in writing this book.

Each quarterly board meeting of the Kauffman Center for Entrepreneurial Leadership at the Ewing Marion Kauffman Foundation these past eight years provided insights into and perspectives on entrepreneurship from an engaged and committed group of entrepreneurial board members. For that I thank Kurt Mueller, president and chairman; Bert Berkley; Pat Cloherty; Bob Compton;

Brant Cotterman; Willie Davis; Mike Herman; Cliff Illig; Audrey MacLean; Bob Rogers; Michie Slaughter; and Lou Smith; and advisors to the board, Tony Mayer and Jeffry Timmons.

At the Center, I have been fortunate to work with a remarkable group of people. I have been proud to know and work with the leadership team in the Entrepreneur Training Institute: Michael Camp, Judith Cone, Trish Costello, Jana Matthews, and Tony Mendes. I thank them and the staff of ETI for making me a better manager and leader.

Some at the Center and Foundation I want to especially acknowledge: Kurt Mueller, who provided the entrepreneurial flexibility for me to complete this book; Michie Slaughter, who recruited me to the Center and from whom I learned about organization development; Steve Roling, who was my first contact with the Center and promised me that it never snowed in Kansas City; my partner in the Center, Marilyn Kourilsky, who knows more about youth entrepreneurship than anyone else in the universe; and Rhonda Holman, who leads our area of public sector and community entrepreneurship.

I'm grateful to my associates at the Center and Foundation for their support, good will, and expertise. I have admired and benefited from the way they kept their knees bent and eyes on the horizon! I especially want to thank Kate Pope Hodel for her talent with communications, Alicia Mitchelson for her administrative skill, and Matt Long for his work on my radio commentaries.

I am indebted to Mary Miller, my associate in the office of the vice president. Her extraordinary competence, unfailing good humor, and concern for others have made her a joy to work with. She has seen this book through all its revisions while handling a myriad of other responsibilities with aplomb. Thank you, Mary.

I appreciate other friends and colleagues who helped shape my understanding of entrepreneurship. George Kozmetsky showed me daily for thirteen years what an entrepreneur does. Out of that came a treasured friendship. I have also learned from the late Gloria Appel, Joe Aragona, Bob Beyster, Umberto Bozzo, Richard Tavener, Bill Strickland, Lee Walker, and many others.

I have appreciated the access that I have had to important organizations of entrepreneurs. The Entrepreneur Of The Year Institute, directed by Ernst & Young, is the preeminent recognition program for entrepreneurs. It has been a pleasure to work with Greg Ericksen, national director of the program. The Young Entrepreneurs' Organization and the Council of Growing Companies are made up of men and women who not only build successful companies but also demonstrate the best values of entrepreneurship. I have enjoyed working with Doug Mellinger, former president of YEO who first introduced me to the organization, and Bob Morgan, president of the Council. Most of entrepreneurs in this book are members of these associations.

I thank Guy Kawasaki for bringing his entrepreneurial spirit, perspective, and experience to the Foreword for this book.

In addition to many of the people already mentioned, Tom Byers, Dale Meyer, and Steve Rogers read and commented on the manuscript. I'm grateful for their comments and suggestions. I hope everyone who reviewed the book will recognize their recommendations and will know that even the ones I chose not to incorporate were valuable in helping me think more carefully about what I wanted to say and how I wanted to say it.

After hearing a speech of mine, Jere Calmes, the former senior editor for business products at Adams Media Corporation, asked if I had ever thought about writing a book based on the talk. Indeed I had. I have appreciated his enthusiasm for the book and benefited from his expertise as editor. I am also grateful for the editorial support of Elizabeth Gilbert.

Most of all, I thank my wife and my two great sons. Judy has been my entrepreneurial partner in life for over thirty years. I loved her at first sight and still can't take my eyes off her. Matthew Wesley and Kevin Raymond are joys to me and have helped me learn how to deal with fatherhood entrepreneurially. How did I get so lucky?

Introduction

Tipping Point

What makes the stories of entrepreneurial achievement so compelling? Is it the daring that seems to lie behind the entrepreneur's decision to launch a venture? The apparent willingness of entrepreneurs to leap before they look? Is it the amazing determination that entrepreneurs sometimes demonstrate in the face of obstacles, setbacks, and catastrophes? The never-say-die attitude that can turn seemingly certain defeat into victory? Is it the wealth and value that entrepreneurs can create? Their ability to start with little or nothing and then somehow magically generate products and profits? Is it that so many examples of entrepreneurial ventures carry elements of comedies and tragedies? That in these attempts at company creation and development lie happiness and disappointment? Each of these elements contributes to making the stories of entrepreneurs not only interesting but also worth learning about and reflecting upon. But something deeper, at least for me, is also at work in the entrepreneurial process. Entrepreneurs truly believe in their ability to influence events, in their capacity to direct destiny, in their power to shape the future.

Evidence abounds that entrepreneurs do indeed create their own futures. Michael Dell builds a multibillion-dollar computer company from his apartment as a nineteen-year-old student at the University of Texas at Austin. Debbi Fields establishes an international cookie company because she loved baking cookies as a child. Dan Dye and Mark Beckloff set up a nationwide bakery for dogs after developing recipes for healthy snacks for pets in the middle of the night in their kitchen at home. Jack Stack turns a desperate situation at a failing manufacturing plant into one of the best companies to work for in America. Jeff Bezos revolutionizes the book-selling business by putting his bookstore online. The list is literally endless. Entrepreneurs believe in their own futures.

But where does this belief come from? What are the elements in the makeup of the entrepreneur that help explain this confidence? How can we understand what makes entrepreneurs tick?

Era of Entrepreneurship

We are in the midst of the greatest era of entrepreneurship in American history. The number of entrepreneurs—men and women, young and old—who are launching and building companies today is unprecedented. Large companies are trying to become more like smaller, entrepreneurial firms. New, growth enterprises are the engines of job and wealth creation. The scope, diversity, and range of entrepreneurial opportunities are truly amazing. We have reached a "tipping point" of entrepreneurial creativity, innovation, and initiative that has altered the landscape of American society and economy.

Malcolm Gladwell in his provocative book, *The Tipping Point*, describes the forces that result in a dramatic moment in the life of an idea or movement when everything can change all at once. "The Tipping Point is the moment of critical mass, the threshold, the boiling point." Gladwell maintains that a major trend emerges like an epidemic and that ideas and behaviors can spread just as viruses do. He points to three characteristics that define these kinds of epidemics in action. First, they are the result of contagious behavior. In other words, people get "infected" with the behavior and thus duplicate the behavior, which serves to infect others. Second, little changes can have big effects. Seemingly small, incremental developments can lead to enormous shifts in how people act. Third, change happens fast; it doesn't build slowly and steadily. Thus, the possibility of sudden change is at the center of the idea of the tipping point.

Entrepreneurship has reached the tipping point. As a result, we are seeing an entrepreneurial revolution that reaches from the inner city to the most affluent suburbs, that encompasses every ethnic group and both genders, that includes the young and the old, and that offers genuine hope and choice to all classes of Americans.

Types of Entrepreneurs

To appreciate the range and impact of this entrepreneurial revolution, it's important to recognize that there are different kinds of entrepreneurs—aspiring, lifestyle, and growth.

Aspiring entrepreneurs are the entrepreneur wannabes. They dream of starting a business; they hope for the chance to be their own bosses. But they have not yet made the leap from current employment into the uncertain and potentially surprising chaos of startup. There are a lot of aspiring entrepreneurs in our country today:

- The 1999 Global Entrepreneurship Monitor report found that at any point in time, 8.5 percent of the U.S. adult population (one in every twelve people) are starting new businesses—the highest startup rate among the ten countries studied.
- Annual National Gallup surveys of U.S. high school students have found that seven out of 10 students want to own their own businesses in their adult years. Six in 10 female, seven in 10 Hispanic, and eight in 10 African-American high school students are interested in starting a business.
- Over 1,400 colleges and universities now offer courses, programs, and internships in entrepreneurship. Many have entrepreneurship centers, degree concentrations in entrepreneurship, and new curriculum offerings in areas like e-commerce.
- Entrepreneurship education programs for youngsters in the K–12 age groups now exist in more than 40 states. The Mini-Society® entrepreneurship curriculum has been

accepted by the U.S. Department of Education's National Diffusion Network as effective in both knowledge acquisition and improving attitudes toward school and learning.

Lifestyle entrepreneurs are those who have developed an enterprise that fits their individual circumstances and style of life. Their basic intention is to earn an income for themselves and their families. These entrepreneurs have been referred to as small businesses or mom-and-pop shops. I don't like either of these latter terms. "Small business" does not capture the fight for survival, the innovation, and the dynamism that are part of any entrepreneurial venture, and "mom-and-pop" seems denigrating to the drive and work that are necessary in any enterprise.

Lifestyle entrepreneurs develop ventures that are essential to a community's well being. Today, we have more customization, variety, and selection because of the increase in lifestyle enterprises than ever before. There are more bakeries, coffee shops, and jewelry stores than ever. There are more breweries, restaurants, and grocery stores. The Internet has spurred a plethora of software developers, retail operations, and service providers. There is simply more diversity because of the dramatic rise in the number of lifestyle entrepreneurs:

- Over 770,000 businesses were incorporated in 1998. Since 1990, more than 600,000 businesses have been incorporated each year. This compares to approximately 100,000 a year in the 1950s.
- In 1998, there were 41 million SOHO businesses (Small Office/Home Office) with a forecast to 51 million by 2002.

Roughly half of home-based businesses are service firms, from consulting practices to graphic design. The rest: sales (17 percent), technical and administrative support (15 percent), repair service (11 percent), and the arts (5 percent).

▌ In 1999, 9.1 million women-owned companies (38 percent of all firms in the United States) employed 27.5 million people and generated nearly $4 trillion in sales. Employment in U.S. women-owned firms with 100 or more employees has expanded six times faster than all firms in the economy. As of 1996, women of color owned one in eight women-owned firms in the United States. The number of minority women-owned firms increased by 153 percent between 1987 and 1996—three times faster than the overall rate.

▌ In 1997, there were an estimated 3.5 million minority-owned businesses in the United States, increasing 168 percent from 1987. Hispanic-owned businesses accounted for 1.4 million, followed by Asian-owned (1.1 million) and Black-owned (880,000). All experienced dramatic growth compared to 1987.

Growth entrepreneurs have both the desire and ability to grow as fast and as large as possible. These firms are the most dynamic job generators in the American economy:

▌ The gazelles of this entrepreneurial stampede, as David Birch at Cognetics Inc. in Cambridge, Massachusetts, calls them, are increasing as well. By his reckoning, there are roughly 300,000 U.S. companies with more than 50 employees that are growing at more than 20 percent per year. And a smaller percentage, including Microsoft and Dell Computer Corporation, are growing even faster and are shaping a very different makeup to the *Fortune* 500.

I Associations and affiliations of growth entrepreneurs have been forming at local, regional, and national levels. The American Entrepreneurs for Economic Growth boasts a membership of over 8,000 firms with more than 3 million employees. The 6,000 members of the Entrepreneur Of The Year Institute have revenues of over $200 billion and employment of over 2 million while growing collectively at an estimated rate of 150,000 jobs per year. The Young Entrepreneurs' Organization has over 3,000 members who are under 40 years of age with a minimum of $1 million in annual revenues. The Council of Growing Companies claims over 1,500 members, each of whom has a minimum of $3 million in annual revenues.

I Roughly 80 percent of the current *Forbes* 400 list of wealthiest Americans are first-generation entrepreneurs whose most common characteristic can be summed up as "started with little or nothing and built major enterprises creating enormous wealth." This entrepreneurial dominance of the list of America's wealthiest has held for every year since the magazine started publishing the list in 1982.

A New Workforce

My dad worked for the Ford Motor Company at its engine plant on Brookpark Road in Cleveland, Ohio, for thirty-eight years before he retired in the early 1990s. He did his job, as directed by management and approved by the union, every working day for each of those nearly four decades. In return, he was assured a good wage, benefits, job security, and a comfortable retirement. He was among the last of a breed of workers in America.

I recall what that kind of work was like. I did it for a while as I worked my way through college in the late 1960s. My job was to tighten three bolts on the engine blocks as they went by every 18 seconds on the assembly line. The worker on my left put the bolts on. I tightened them with an air gun. And the worker on my right wiped them clean with a cloth. On one occasion, the three of us decided to combine the three jobs into one so that we worked a half-hour and had an hour off. It was easy to do. Except that we were almost fired for trying this. We thought that we were increasing productivity—having one person do the job of three. But the management foreman lambasted us for not working, and the union steward told us we were actually creating a case to eliminate two jobs! So back the three of us went—putting on the bolts, tightening them, wiping them clean—for eight hours a day, six days a week.

Neither my Dad nor we understood or cared about how our jobs related to the final automobile that left the complex, much less how we impacted the competitiveness of the company that employed us.

We know that type of workforce is gone forever. But what is replacing it?

My son Matthew is a twenty-one-year-old college student. He has a very different view of work. He does not believe that a big company will provide job security and sees the large corporation as stifling and limiting to what he wants to do. He does not believe that Social Security will be around when he will be old enough to benefit from it. He likes the idea of being his own boss and having more control over his own destiny. He wants to do something worthwhile. He has already had two entrepreneurial ventures that he started, has written a business plan for a restaurant concept that he developed, and served as an intern during his senior year in high school in two entrepreneurial firms (one of which failed and one of which succeeded). He represents a new breed of worker in America.

Dan Pinks, founder of FreeAgentNation.com, would call my son a "free agent." In an age of free agency, work becomes personal, and people seek to do what they love. The new workforce, an entrepreneurial workforce, is more willing to "fly without a net." As a result, people are redefining success, emphasizing authenticity, and pledging loyalty to their teams, networks, and colleagues rather than to organizations.

A Tale of Two Economies

The American economy of free agency reflects Charles Dickens's famous opening line in *A Tale of Two Cities*, "These are the best of times; these are the worst of times." For workers, we have a tale of two economies—the big-company economy and the entrepreneurial economy.

On the one hand, many workers are experiencing enormous dislocation. Traditional values of job security, seniority, and loyalty have been jarred by demands for flexibility, productivity, and performance. Driven by international competitiveness, innovative labor-eliminating technologies, requirements for new kinds of skills and more decentralized, autonomous team approaches to getting the job done, large corporations have dramatically cut employees, changed reward systems, and altered management structures. In other words, they are trying to become more entrepreneurial.

In 1960, about 15 percent of American workers got their paychecks from *Fortune* 500 companies. This percentage grew to a high of about 21 percent in 1970 and stabilized there for about a decade. In 1980, the number of workers in *Fortune* 500 companies began a steady decline so that today less than 9 percent of the workforce is in *Fortune* 500 firms. Since 1980, *Fortune* 500 firms have cut five million jobs. For those people who have been downsized, these companies would more likely be called the "Mis*Fortune* 500." This was illustrated on the cover of the February 25, 1996, issue of *Newsweek* magazine. Under the title of "Corporate Killers" were the photos of four CEOs of *Fortune* 500 companies. Beneath their names, like serial numbers under mug shots, were the number of jobs they had cut: Digital, 20,000; Scott, 11,000; AT&T, 40,000; IBM, 60,000. CEOs of other major corporations were pictured in the article in a type of rogues' gallery with the number of layoffs that each had supervised in red type beneath their pictures. The subtitle on the cover read, "The Public Is Scared as Hell. Is There a Better Way?"

Job-Generating Businesses

Yes, there is. In another sense, these are the best of times for American workers. Since 1980, thirty-four million new jobs have been created. So, who's hiring? Entrepreneurs are hiring. They are generating their own jobs and creating jobs for others.

Small Business Administration data shows that between 1992 and 1996, 11.18 million new jobs were created. All of the net new jobs came from firms with fewer than 500 employees. Microbusinesses with one to four employees created 52 percent of these net new jobs. And jobs created by new firms accounted for about 70 percent of the total employment increase. Large firms with more than 500 employees posted a net loss of nearly 650,000 jobs during this period.

Entrepreneurship is the golden goose of job creation in America. The proliferation of new ventures springs from two factors—one personal and the other structural. Structurally, the United States promotes an environment conducive to enterprise startup and growth. This environment combines market opportunities with infrastructure support (like availability of financing, facilities, tax concessions, and government assistance); access to education; and cultural values that endorse independence and self-reliance, respect those starting companies, and tolerate failure in the enterprise process.

Personally, entrepreneurs have attitude. Jim McGraw, the COO of Marion Laboratories during its dynamic growth years, captured the mental framework of entrepreneurs by declaring, "Attitude determines outcome." The report of the *Global Entrepreneurship Monitor*, a comparative study of entrepreneurship in ten countries, calls this attitude "entrepreneurial capacity." The study declares that, "For an entrepreneurial initiative to occur one must possess the capacity (i.e., the motivation and skill) to take advantage of the opportunity by starting a new firm." The United States has the highest rating of entrepreneurial capacity of any country in the study!

As long as entrepreneurs have the motivation and skill to start companies and as long as American society provides an environment that encourages them to do so, the outcome will be jobs in the entrepreneurial economy.

Looking Ahead

This book is divided into six sections to capture the why and the how of this upsurge in entrepreneurship. Section I on the "Soul of the Entrepreneur" focuses on what accounts for the spirit behind and the drive within entrepreneurs. It addresses the reasons for their internal motivation to start and build an enterprise and for their sense of calling to do something significant. It deals with the issues of passion, purpose, vision, meaning, and optimism that make up the outlook of entrepreneurs.

Section II on the "Secrets of Entrepreneurial Success" discusses the factors that cause some entrepreneurs to flourish while others fall by the wayside. It provides insights and recommendations on what entrepreneurs can do to increase their chances of building and sustaining viable enterprises. It addresses themes of the pursuit of opportunity, proclivity for action, being one's own boss, taking risk, and bringing talent into growing ventures.

Section III examines what entrepreneurs do. "Skills of Entrepreneurs" looks at the specific skills entrepreneurs use to run growing enterprises. It emphasizes networking, selling, leading, learning, building relationships, and planning, and suggests actions that entrepreneurs can take to improve these important skills in themselves.

"Experience of Entrepreneurship," Section IV, provides a sense of what it's really like to be in an entrepreneurial venture. It gives a view from the inside out of what an entrepreneur goes through in starting and running a business. This section shows the subversive nature of the entrepreneurial process, describes the chaotic and ambiguous environment that entrepreneurs can find themselves in, reviews the paradoxical nature of running a growth venture, and addresses the frustrations as well as the opportunities of fundraising.

Section V on "Managing the Dark Side" reveals the painful side of entrepreneurship. It delineates the major personal problems and obstacles that entrepreneurs can encounter in building their businesses, and makes recommendations on what entrepreneurs can do to deal with these. It focuses on failure, burnout, the perception of ruthlessness, being kicked up or out of one's own company, and loneliness.

Perspectives on the "Social Impact of Entrepreneurship" run through Section VI. Themes here include job and wealth creation, building community, ethics and reputation, and education. This section addresses the role that entrepreneurship plays in providing for economic vitality and social well being.

Each section features entrepreneurs whose examples and experiences reflect the issues of that part of the book, and concludes with a profile of an entrepreneur who provides a more in-depth story to tie the various themes of that section together.

Phenomenon of Entrepreneurship

We have reached the tipping point of entrepreneurial activity for some very practical reasons. A combination of pushes and pulls are spurring individuals to try the entrepreneurial route. The pushes may be a loss of job, dissatisfaction with current employment, or the now-or-never feeling that can nag on one's brain. The pulls involve the enticement of a market opportunity, expanding access to customers via the Internet, the availability of capital, the desire for independence, a positive view of the entrepreneur in the media, or the influence of role models who have done it successfully.

In a period that presents both disturbing economic dislocation and appealing opportunity, entrepreneurship is proving to be a truly egalitarian avenue to self-sufficiency and a better life for many. Every entrepreneur who launches a company believes he or she can create his or her own future. This book is about how entrepreneurs do that.

Section I

SOUL OF THE ENTREPRENEUR

1

Mysterious Core

For all we know about balance sheets, income statements, and cash flow accounting; for all of our understanding about marketing strategies, tactics, and techniques; and for everything we have learned about management principles and practices, there remains something essential, yet mysterious, at the core of entrepreneurship. It is so mysterious that we cannot see it or touch it; yet we feel it and know it exists. It cannot be mined, manufactured, or bought; yet it can be discovered. Its source is invisible; yet its results are tangible and measurable.

This mysterious core is so powerful that it can make the remarkable appear ordinary, so contagious that it can spread like wildfire from one to another in an organization, and so persuasive that it can transform doubt and uncertainty into conviction.

Fire in the Belly

This mysterious core is passion. Passion is the essence of entrepreneurship. In the entrepreneur, it is described as drive—the determined, optimistic, persistent desire to succeed at one's own venture. It is the "fire in the belly" that makes the improbable possible. It is the wellspring of the entrepreneur's Ripkinesque stick-to-itiveness to always, always, show up for the game. Passion is the basis of Peter Drucker's astute observation that "Whenever anything is being accomplished, it is being done . . . by a monomaniac with a mission."

It's hard to stop someone who is on a mission. The late Michael Chowdry came to the United States from Pakistan via London in the mid-1970s at the age of 22 with a desire to be successful at something. Through an aviation program at the University of Minnesota, he fell in love with flying and earned his Certified Flight Instructor license, after which he began to do anything that would keep him in the air—crop dusting, instructing, even performing aerobatics. He sold Piper airplanes and managed a commuter airline before turning his passion into a major entrepreneurial venture.

Chowdry saw a need for low-cost, long-distance airline cargo carriers as part of the emerging direction of global commerce. He founded Atlas Air in 1992 to outsource Boeing 747 aircraft to carry cargo all over the world. The company owns the aircraft, crew, maintenance, and insurance, known as ACMI in the industry. Customers include leading international airline carriers that bear all other operating costs, including fuel, cargo, and ground handling. This unique business model has allowed Atlas to control 80 percent of the world's ACMI cargo and become the third largest cargo carrier in the world for revenue-tons carried. The company went public in 1997. On the day of the IPO, the proudest day in his life, Chowdry, with his young son at his side, heard the sound of success as he rang the bell on the New York Stock Exchange. In addition to building a fast-growth company, Chowdry used to get in the cockpit of one of his 747s, a telling symbol of how one's passion can become one's business.

But what is passion? What is its common cause? Where does it come from? Who has it?

Zealous Pursuit

Passion is the enthusiasm, joy, and zeal that come from the energetic and unflagging pursuit of a worthy, challenging, and uplifting purpose.

Richard and James Cabela's love of the great outdoors led the brothers to turn a hobby of hand tying fishing flies into Cabela's Incorporated, an international retail organization in the outdoor gear industry distributing 65 million catalogs in 120 countries. Peter Johnson set out to transform the drug discovery process from an exercise in serendipity into an engineering discipline and built Agouron Pharmaceuticals. Agouron developed VIRACEPT, a protease inhibitor for the treatment of those with AIDS, which the company provides free of charge to patients with the greatest need and the least ability to pay, as well as to any child in the United States not covered by insurance. William Kubly combined his dedication to architecture with his avid interest in golf to build Landscapes Unlimited into one of the largest and most respected golf course construction and renovation companies in the country. David Bohnett wanted to provide people on the World Wide Web with a sense of home and community. He established GeoCities in 1994 to allow members, called Homesteaders, to create their own personal Web sites and to interact with other members in any one of 41 different interest areas, called Neighborhoods, for free. In 1999, Yahoo! acquired GeoCities, now the fourth most popular site on the Internet.

Passion is intrinsic. Its locus is inside each one of us. So it does not have to be, in fact cannot be, instilled or motivated into somebody else. It must only be given the freedom and opportunity to emerge.

Passion emerges when one has the freedom and opportunity to pursue one's dream—to do what one loves to do. To be human is to dream—to dream about self-improvement, self-fulfillment, and self-actualization. The significance of this is that there is no correlation between dreaming and one's environment. A person in the inner city who has never gone mountain climbing can still dream about scaling Mr. Everest. A farm boy from Missouri who loved to sell pharmaceuticals to physicians could dream about building a great company—as Ewing Kauffman did in building Marion Laboratories from an initial investment of $5,000 in the basement of his house to an organization valued at $6.5 billion. And a successful research scientist can choose to give up a promising career in a large corporation to pursue his dream to build an employee-owned high-technology company, as Bob Beyster did in 1969 to start SAIC and shape it into a $5 billion per year enterprise.

The real challenge for the entrepreneur in building a successful company is to find ways to turn passion into practice, to transform dreams into realities, not only for himself or herself, but for everyone in the organization. The real challenge is to find ways for everyone to buy in, practically and emotionally, to his or her dream, indeed, to make his or her dream part of everyone else's dreams.

The ability to do that is the real mark of leadership for entrepreneurs who build great companies.

2

Mighty Purpose

How does an entrepreneur with a dream get others to buy into it, to share his or her commitment to it?

I am convinced that commitment, real commitment, comes from a feeling of ownership about what one is doing. If you think about it, each of us owns our own dreams. They are completely ours. These dreams give purpose to our lives. A sausage manufacturer in Kansas City beams when talking about the quality and taste of his sausage; a software developer in Austin, Texas, radiates when describing her product; and a young designer of CD-ROMs in San Diego glows when showing off his latest innovation.

George Bernard Shaw provided the essential insight into one's purpose. He said, "This is the true joy in life, the being used for a purpose recognized by yourself as a mighty one."

Secret of Life

This same message of mighty purpose was conveyed in the delightful movie *City Slickers*. The range-hardened cowboy, played by Jack Palance, tells city slicker Billy Crystal that he has learned the meaning of life. When Crystal asks what it is, Palance holds up one finger and says, "This is the secret of life." When Crystal asks what that one thing is, Palance tells him, "That's for you to decide!"

George DeVries decided to improve the health-care options available to people. He saw patients extremely satisfied with chiropractic treatment and believed that employers would begin to request benefits for their employees. Consequently, he started American Health Specialty, Inc. in 1987, when he was 28 years old, out of the second bedroom of his condominium with a few thousand dollars. Today, AHS is the nation's largest health service organization for complementary and alternative health care, covering 25 million members and contracting with over 19,000 providers with over $75 million in annual revenues.

In their book, *Leading with Soul*, Lee Bolman and Terry Deal, two scholars on leadership and organization development, argue that effective leadership is a relationship rooted in community—a community of shared values and beliefs that results in commitment. They write:

> *The heart of leadership lies in the hearts of leaders. We fool ourselves, thinking that sheer bravado or sophisticated analytic techniques could respond to our deepest concerns. . . . Leading with soul returns us to ancient spiritual basics—reclaiming the enduring human capacity that gives our lives purpose and passion.*

To reclaim that capacity, they recommend that leaders provide others with power and authorship—in other words, they must own, monetarily and/or emotionally, what they do.

Ironically, there is a paradox at work here. The leader must confront his or her fear of letting go, of being out of complete control. Holding on too tightly to anything actually risks losing everything. So the practical issue for the leader of an entrepreneurial organization is how to let go, but hold on at the same time. Effective entrepreneurs let go of responsibility, and sometimes ownership of a portion of the company, but hold on to their mighty purpose.

During its growth, the Herman Miller Company promoted a management philosophy that companies, like the people who compose them, are always in a state of becoming. Therefore, the workplace must be a place of high-quality relationships. In other words, it must be a community where relationships are just as important as structure. This approach made the firm the most productive in terms of net income per employee and placed it on *Fortune*'s list of most-admired companies.

Responsibility to Perform

Ownership, however, is a two-way street. Those who own have the responsibility to perform. Fulfillment and actualization of dreams come only with performance and achievement.

The buying-in to an entrepreneur's dream has both emotional and practical outcomes. First, it allows each person in the organization to be part of something larger than himself or herself—to take pride in something well and remarkably accomplished.

In their book, *Breakthroughs*, John Ketteringham and P. Ranganath Nayak, two McKinsey & Company consultants, documented several great commercial success stories and found that the common element among all the participants in each of them was the feeling of accomplishment that came from being part of a mighty purpose.

Second, buying in to an entrepreneur's dream provides the possibility of pursuing one's own dreams—whether that be building a home in the mountains, putting the kids through college, traveling around the world, or investing in other companies—by participating in the wealth-creation process.

Aelred Kurtenbach set out to build a world-class company, primarily with the talents and hard work of South Dakota's college graduates. To fulfill his mighty purpose, he reimburses tuition, fees, and costs of books for employees; holds college courses in his facility; provides scholarships for local college and high school students; sponsors an engineering training program to assist South Dakota graduate engineering students working toward graduate degrees; and provides cash awards to students to help start new South Dakota businesses. As a result, his company, Daktronics, headquartered in Brookings, South Dakota, has become a leading designer and manufacturer of computer programmable displays, electronic scoreboards, and voting systems, with revenues of over $120 million in 2000.

The great Supreme Court Justice Oliver Wendell Holmes observed, "What lies behind us and what lies before us are tiny matters compared to what lies within us." And what lies within every successful entrepreneur is a mighty purpose.

3

Force Fields

B elieving is seeing! This is the entrepreneur's twist on the adage
that describes the most important and compelling element of
great entrepreneurs. Great entrepreneurs bring powerful, embracing
visions to their enterprises. They first believe, and then they see.

In the first major, national study on leadership skills of entrepreneurs conducted by the Center for Creative Leadership, the
key predictor of success in entrepreneurial ventures was found to
be the vision of the entrepreneur. More important than money,
more critical than management, more essential than markets,
vision is the driving and sustaining force that determines the
growth and vitality—the very life—of an entrepreneurial venture
across all stages of development. The reverse is also true. Companies without vision collapse.

Vision can take unconventional form in entrepreneurial ventures. Jack Stack and the other 119 employee-owners of Springfield ReManufacturing Corporation (SRC) in Springfield, Missouri, shaped a clear, concise, and convincing vision for their company when they took over a firm in desperate straits over a decade ago. Faced with the burden of an 89:1 debit-to-equity ratio, a labor versus management mindset, and an environment of uncertainty and doubt, they agreed: "Don't run out of cash and don't destroy from within." They never have.

This practical but compelling vision built a culture of education, open information about all financials, ownership, teamwork, and performance that has made SRC one of the 100 best companies to work for in America.

But what is vision? If it is so critical to success, how does it influence what an organization becomes and what it does?

Organizational Sixth Sense

I am convinced that vision is more than a destination or a desired stage of development; that it is more than a picture of a preferred future; that it is more than a dream of where one wants to be.

Vision is the organizational sixth sense that tells us why we make a difference in this world. It is the real but unseen fabric of connections that nurture and sustain values. It is the pulse of the organizational body that reaffirms relationships and directs behavior.

In the *Star Wars* saga, the Jedi Knights keep reminding one another, "May the Force be with you." And in crisis situations, in moments of the greatest uncertainty, difficulty, and danger, they rely on this force to guide their thinking and direct their behavior. In the dramatic final scene of the first film, Luke Skywalker turned away from the science and technology that surrounded him and put his trust in something deeper and more powerful—a force that he could not see, but nevertheless felt and tapped into.

Is this force just the stuff of movies? I don't think so. Margaret Wheatley, an organization scholar, in her important book, *Leadership and the New Science*, relates the concept of force fields in nature (such as the force of gravity and magnetic fields) to organizational leadership. We know that these force fields exist, that they exert powerful influences over objects with which they come in contact, but that they are invisible. She says, "I have come to understand organizational vision as a field—a force of unseen connections that influence employees' behavior—rather than as an evocative message about some desired future state."

Vision, in this context, is the organizational energy that charges behavior, fuels direction, and catalyzes change. For vision to be genuinely powerful in organizations, it must be personal, positive, emotional, and larger than ourselves. Vision thus impacts an organization when people buy into and act upon the invisible.

Uncle Harry

Timothy Hoeksema had a vision to build an airline that would provide "the best care in the air." He would create an airline that would provide first-class service for every passenger. Starting a small shuttle fleet in 1984 for executives at Kimberly-Clark, the paper products manufacturer, he spun Midwest Express off as a separate publicly held company in 1995. From the start, he went against the cost-cutting, no-frills movement of the airline industry. He was convinced that an airline that provided unparalleled service and unmatched quality could be successful. "There were a lot of people who thought I was a little crazy," he says. "Then when I started describing the plans in detail, people thought I was a lot crazy!"

He envisioned an airline with no middle seats, providing two larger, leather, luxurious seats for more space and comfort for passengers. He would provide gourmet meals with wine and champagne, cookies baked fresh in the air, and other things like complimentary newspapers at the gates. Every employee would have to be committed to doing whatever was necessary to make a passenger's flight an enjoyable, even memorable, experience. Consequently, he proceeded to do the unconventional to create a culture that would make the vision a reality.

Today, Hoeksema spends twice the industry average on meals, makes sure employees are customer oriented through orientation and training, and has everyone—leadership, management, and employees—sign commitment pledges that are promises of what they will do for customers and for each other. From 1992 to 1999, *Consumer Reports* ranked Midwest Express the nation's best airline in terms of customer satisfaction. Earnings for 1998 were $36 million on revenues of $389 million.

Hoeksema tells the story of Uncle Harry, a story that each of the more than 3,000 employees of Midwest Express knows and one that reflects how vision affects performance. During the great floods in the Midwest a few years ago, two men were trapped on top of a house as water engulfed the second floor of the dwelling.

As they waited for rescue, one of the men noticed a hat that seemed to be floating on the surface of the water not far from the house. On further observation, he realized that the hat was moving in one direction, would stop and then move back in the opposite direction. This back-and-forth movement of the hat continued for some time. Finally, he drew the attention of the second man to this unusual movement and wondered what it could be. The second man replied, "Oh, that's Uncle Harry. He promised to mow the lawn come hell or high water!" That's exactly the attitude and action to which employees of Midwest Express are committed to provide "the best care in the air."

Successful entrepreneurs create force fields from their visions. These fields are felt but unseen structures that occupy organizational space; they become known through their affects on the conduct of those in the company. The more sincere the belief in the vision, the more consistent the messages about the vision, and the more coherent the behavior around the vision, the greater the force of the field on everyone in the organization who bumps up against it.

4

Creating Meaning

Today's entrepreneurs are seeking a different kind of business life, one richer in meaning for themselves, their employees, and their customers. They are building enterprises that are as much values based, as product or service driven. Jim Collins, the co-author of *Built to Last*, has observed that there is a legion of businesspeople who "are hungry to build something of enduring character on a fundamental set of values they can be proud of." He contends, "We're going to see companies increasingly assume that what they stand for in an enduring sense is more important than what they sell." I'm convinced this is true.

What You Stand For

Rick Krska, who leads LaserCycle, a fast-growth company that remanufactures toner and inkjet cartridges in Lenexa, Kansas, reflects this movement to meaning:

> *We are working on, and continue to work on, building a company that is about benefiting all of us as we make something here. And some of the words that we use around here are probably not words that are used in normal, everyday business. One of the things that I talk about is that I want us to love each other and care about each other. I care about you, I care about your family. I want you to do well, and I line up with people when I feel that they have an interest in me like that. And I know they feel the same way in return. So we're trying to build a company that is based on all of us treating each other well, being good to each other, helping each other, and I feel like that focus almost has to be there first.*

Krska's values of "treating each other well, being good to each other, helping each other" have created an environment that has meaning for him and his employees. One result is extraordinary performance and rapid growth. "Love" and "care" may not be heard regularly in business today, but I believe that we will hear them more in the future.

When Ewing Kauffman's pharmaceutical company, Marion Laboratories, was sold to Merrell Dow in 1989 for $6.5 billion, the Marion culture changed. Many associates left the new company that resulted from the merger. But they did not want to leave what Marion had meant to them. Consequently, they created an alumni association of over 700 former associates to stay in touch with one another—a telling example of an entrepreneur's ability to create meaning.

Danny O'Neill is building The Roasterie, a fast-growth gourmet coffee company in Kansas City, Missouri. He is determined to make and distribute only the very best coffee available anywhere in the world. So he often pays far more than competitors, but he refuses to sacrifice quality, even when that would give him a better short-term bottom line. When I visited his manufacturing facility, I learned what coffee meant for him.

He told me that when he sees a coffee bean on the floor of his plant, "It rips out my soul!" He explained how he had to make every employee feel the same way he does. So he explained to them what it's like to pick coffee beans; he showed them how it takes 2,000 beans to make one pound of coffee; he told them how many fingers of how many families touch those beans and depend on those beans for their livelihoods before they ever reach their plant; he had them taste the difference between their coffee and other coffees; and he explained how their success depends on how well they take care of each and every bean. There are no beans on Danny O'Neill's manufacturing floor!

Aribians

The first issue to consider in identifying promising companies is to determine whether the entrepreneurs who lead them can clearly define and articulate the company's (and their own) core purpose and values. Do the people in the company understand the basic rules of the company and buy into them? Has the entrepreneur demonstrated the ability to inspire through words and actions? Is there a shared sense of the values of the organization?

A shared sense of values is evident at Ariba, which develops technology to power internal procurement processes for corporations to facilitate commerce over the Internet. By leveraging the Internet for more efficient business-to-business commerce, CEO Keith Krach has built a fast-growth firm with over 1,000 employees and $45 million in revenues in 1999. His rules for Ariba are clear: truth and integrity; there are no bad ideas; raise the standards of performance; team first, functional specialist second; and hire the best people, even if they are better than you are. The result is that employees at the company view themselves as "Aribians," as though they were inhabitants of a unique and favored planet of their own making.

By creating meaning, entrepreneurs inspire others. They do so primarily by expressing effectively, and demonstrating through their own example, the values that they stand for.

5

The Universal Characteristic

Entrepreneurs are remarkably diverse. Despite the extensive amount of research that has focused on the traits or characteristics of entrepreneurs, no clear set of traits or characteristics applies to all entrepreneurs. In fact, the attempt to identify a specific set of characteristics or to define a specific psychological profile to predict who will be a successful entrepreneur has proved to be a generally frustrating and unsuccessful endeavor.

In reading hundreds of business plans, in my consulting on entrepreneurial ventures, and in my teaching of entrepreneurship, I have observed something remarkable and universal about the entrepreneurial process. In fact, it is the only characteristic, I believe, that is common to every plan, the only element that applies to all entrepreneurs without exception, no matter their age, gender, background, or experience. Every entrepreneur believes his or her company will succeed. Think about that. No business plan ever predicts failure. No entrepreneur ever tells a potential investor, "You're sure to lose your shirt on this one!" No projection of revenues ever presents an upside-down hockey stick.

Every entrepreneur is convinced that the future has to be better than the past and will certainly improve upon the present. This belief in the future, this sense of the possibilities of things, makes the impossible probable and the probable likely in entrepreneurial ventures.

Entrepreneurship thus provides a secret weapon against apathy and anger. It presents an ace in the hole for anyone who wants to build an enterprise. As inveterate optimists, entrepreneurs usually don't know what they can't do. This optimism, this belief in the possible, is a remarkably potent resource for overcoming obstacles.

Is this a Pollyanna approach to enterprise? Not at all.

Psychologist Martin Seligman in his classic book, *Learned Optimism*, conducted groundbreaking work on optimism and success. He found that depressed people tend to be more realistic than optimistic ones. But optimists, even when their good cheer is unwarranted, accomplished more. The more difficult the task and the greater the pressure, the more important optimism became to the success of any endeavor.

Jonathan Coon is the co-founder, president, and CEO of 1-800-CONTACTS. He started his entrepreneurial career as a student selling contact lenses to other college students to obtain contacts for himself and to help pay for college expenses.

After writing a business plan, he launched 1-800-CONTACTS in 1995 with his partner John Nichols. It follows his ideal business model: strong cash flow, easy distribution, and a built-in repeat order potential of a disposable product. Today, the company is the largest direct-to-consumer contact lens seller in the world with revenues of over $125 million. Coon's philosophy, which he communicates to his employees, represents the attitude of successful entrepreneurs: "No Limits: Don't be satisfied with mediocrity or the status quo. If someone says it's not possible, do it anyway." He did.

I'm reminded of the entrepreneur who had not succeeded at several ventures and was now seeking money from an investor for yet another enterprise. She was trying to persuade the wary investor of the viability of her technology, the huge market for the product, and the certain high return on his investment. The investor saw her enthusiasm but remained skeptical. In trying to be kind, the investor remarked that the entrepreneur had a number of blemishes in her past, to which the entrepreneur replied, "That may be true, but my future is spotless!"

Entrepreneurs, who start and build companies, remind all of us that our futures are spotless as well.

6

Long Shots

A private investor recently told a friend of mine who is starting a company that her firm has one chance in a thousand of succeeding. Although this assessment depressed her, I reminded her that longer shots than this have succeed.

Beating the Odds

Venture capitalists refused to fund Michael Dell, believing that no nineteen-year-old could ever build a fast-growth computer company. Now they wish that they had a small percentage of what has become the most successful stock of the 1990s.

Debbi Fields's husband told her that starting a cookie company was the "dumbest" idea he had ever heard of. Three years later, she hired him into Mrs. Fields Cookies.

Bank after bank rejected Jack Stack's request to provide capital for Springfield ReManufacturing Corporation. Now banks clamor for SRC's business since it has become one of the best companies to work for in America.

And sages predicted that Dan Dye and Mark Beckloff, two business novices, could never build a viable enterprise around the concept of selling healthy snacks for dogs. Now Three Dog Bakery is doing $10 million a year with plans to go public.

Real Long Shots

Long shots all. But there are even longer shots. Power Ball odds are 80 million to one. The chances of winning $1 million dollars in the McDonald's Monopoly game are 89 million to one. And the odds of winning $2 million instantly by finding that package of all red M&Ms were 460 million to one.

In fact, starting and building a successful company is a lot more likely and safer than many other events that we could encounter. The odds of being struck by lightning are one in 600,000; getting injured in an elevator ride, one in 6 million; dying in an earthquake, one in 11 million; dying from snake bite, one in 36 million; and being attacked by a shark, one in 60 million.

How to Lower the Odds

I advised my friend to find creative ways to lower the odds so that her chances of success increase.

▎ *Write a good business plan.* A plan is not just a writing exercise. It's a sanity check for the entrepreneur, a financial tool for raising capital, and a planning tool for running the company.

▎ *Set up an advisory board.* A board brings talent into the company by identifying people—like lawyers, accountants, marketing professionals, academics, and successful businesspeople—who share their wisdom and experience, and who provide a sounding board for the entrepreneur.

▎ *Find a mentor.* Locate someone with been-there, done-that experience who cares about you and your company, and who is willing to spend some time helping solve problems. Someone who will listen and then provide constructive feedback is an invaluable resource for building a company.

▎ *Build a network.* Develop links and associations with as broad a group of people as possible. Expand your electronic Rolodex. By developing a diverse, heterogeneous, and extensive list of contacts, entrepreneurs expand their access to resources and to problem solvers.

▎ *Learn.* Be proactive in learning as much as you can about running a business. Take classes, like the Kauffman Center's Fast-Trac, participate in outreach programs at universities near you, and go to events, like breakfast meetings sponsored by chambers of commerce or Entrepreneurship Expos. Successful entrepreneurs are exceptional learners.

Almost a Sure Thing

I told my friend to take heart. If other entrepreneurs who are told in one way or another that they're crazy, that their ideas will never work, that no one will finance their enterprises, that they can't succeed—still find ways to build thriving companies, then she can, too. And if she can avoid being struck by lightning, crashing in an elevator, collapsing in an earthquake, getting bit by a snake and chased by Jaws, then she just might make that doubting investor wish he had a stake in her company.

When you think of long shots this way, one chance in a thousand is almost a sure thing!

7

PROFILE:
Company Personas

They started in their kitchen with a wooden spoon, a rolling pin, and a biscuit cutter that the mother of one of them had put in his Christmas stocking in 1989 as a stocking stuffer. After finishing their day jobs, they would work until midnight and then put in 16 hours on Saturdays and Sundays testing recipes, baking biscuits, and sampling the results. Hour after hour, batch after batch, they kneaded dough, experimented with ingredients, and juggled measurements. They tossed out flop after flop until they got the flavors, textures, and appearances just right. Mark Beckloff and Dan Dye were on a mission. They were determined "to bake the best dog biscuit the civilized world had ever known."

Mark and Dan loved dogs. What better calling in life than to bring to every dog in the galaxy wholesome, all natural, fresh-baked dog treats. So with no money but with unbridled enthusiasm, they set out to produce the best-tasting, healthiest dog treats possible on their kitchen counters. They had three official taste testers at their sides ready to try every sample: Sarah Jean, a black Lab mix; Dottie, a Dalmatian; and Gracie, an albino Great Dane. This was the start of Three Dog Bakery—A Bakery for Dogs in Kansas City, Missouri.

Eventually they were baking Banana Mutt Cookies, Great Danish Crunchies, Pavlov's Punkin' Bread, CollieFlowers, and PupCakes to which their taste testers had given their tail-wagging approval. They set up tables of their products at dog shows and began to get orders on their answering machine. They baked and cut biscuits day and night to try to keep up with orders. Mark was the first to quit his day job to devote full time to the business. Then Dan quit his. They did not take a single day off work for two years. They were filling orders as fast as they could—10 bags here, 20 bags there. But they soon needed more room, another oven, and additional help. So they moved into their first leased space, paying $300 a month, wondering if they could make enough money to cover their costs.

The company continued to grow, so they made a second move to a vacated bakery shop in Weston, Missouri, north of Kansas City. Now they not only had genuine bakery equipment, but also a real showroom with glass cases to display their products—the world's first formal bakery for dogs! This was their dream actually coming true.

They were running a real business now, but realized something important. They really didn't know what they were doing. They had no business plan and were, like many other entrepreneurs, making things up as they went along. How could they increase cash flow? How should they market their product? What kind of talent should they hire next? Consequently, they took an entrepreneur development course called FastTrac in the spring of 1993. They wrote their first business plan, created financial pro-formas and projections, detailed manufacturing requirements, and outlined marketing strategies and tactics. They said, "The best money we ever spent as a company was the tuition we paid to participate in this course."

Then two key events occurred in the growth of the company. They were featured in the *Wall Street Journal* when a stringer for the paper learned about the venture after stopping in to buy treats for his dog. The headline read: "Some of the Puns Are Half-Baked, And the Place Is Going to the Dogs." Suddenly, the phone didn't stop ringing. Other media wanted stories. They appeared on morning television shows and even made an appearance on *Oprah*. Mark and Dan were not only getting attention, they were learning that they had a gift for marketing! They also learned that they needed more money.

That's when Bill Reisler, a venture capitalist with Kansas City Equity Partners, walked into their store to buy treats for his dog. Yogi Berra said, "You can observe a lot just by watching." What Bill observed was a lot of people buying dog treats. "Afterwards," he said, "I called them up because I was sure that there was something that could be done in a bigger way." Kansas City Equity Partners eventually invested approximately a million dollars for about half of the company. Dan said, "We did what we had to do to keep things going." Mark said, "We would rather own a smaller percentage of a huge company than 100 percent of a small company."

Now venture backed, they began to scale up operations, expanding a catalog and mail-order business. They created a unique direct-mail database—mailing directly to the actual dogs when possible! They were still keeping their enterprise fun! And they were coming to the attention of others.

In 1996, PETsMART called them. The nationwide chain of pet stores was looking for a concept that would help differentiate them from their competitors. The company liked the idea of a bakery for dogs in their stores, so it established a strategic alliance with Three Dog Bakery. PETsMART invested a half-million dollars for 10 percent of the company and agreed to set up bakery operations in their stores. According to Dan, the arrangement was "the culmination of a six-year dream." The deal "turns us from a little company to a big company almost overnight." To try to keep up with demand, Three Dog Bakery went to three shifts running 24 hours a day.

Today, Three Dog Bakery continues to grow. Dan and Mark are the personas of the company. Internally, they reinforce the commitment of their firm to "bake the best dog treats on the planet and to get them to as many dogs as possible." Externally, they are masters of marketing, promoting the firm through presentations, books, and television (they have a cable show on food for dogs). The company now has a new president and CEO, an experienced manager who has been involved with other fast-growth ventures, who oversees the operations of the company. PETsMART continues to build Three Dog Bakeries in their stores. With over $10 million in annual revenues and over 150 employees, the company is developing plans to go public and is looking to expand internationally.

As Mark and Dan looked back over their experience, they said in their book, *Short Tails and Treats from Three Dog Bakery*, "We feel like we have been through an emotional wringer. We have experienced the highest of the highs and the lowest of lows. Our personal lives have been closely intertwined with our business." Their advice to other entrepreneurs reflects their own optimism and commitment: "If you are strong enough and brave enough to follow your true heart's desire, and if you do your absolute, passionate best and believe in yourself, you'll achieve everything that you want." They did and have.

SECRETS OF ENTREPRENEURIAL SUCCESS

8

The Bisociative Thinker

How do entrepreneurs keep coming up with successful business concepts? What is it in the mind of the entrepreneur that recognizes opportunities that others miss?

Entrepreneurs demonstrate an uncanny knack to see things in the marketplace that others don't see and then exploit them. This ability to recognize and pursue opportunity is the most fascinating and fundamental aspect of entrepreneurial success, and one of the least understood phenomenons of the entrepreneurial process.

An idea is always at the center of an opportunity, but not all ideas are opportunities. Some ideas have value only in the mind of the inventor or initiator of the idea. An opportunity is an idea that provides genuine value in the minds of others. Therefore, an opportunity is customer driven. It is rooted in meeting a real need or solving a real problem in the marketplace or in creating a demand in the mind of the consumer. Effective entrepreneurs thus understand the environment of their target market. They come to know the desires, concerns, or problems of their customers; find ways to address them; and then provide real benefits that satisfy those desires, concerns, or problems.

Pursuit of Opportunity

Howard Stevenson and the other entrepreneurship faculty at the Harvard Business School have developed the most widely accepted definition of entrepreneurship as "the pursuit of opportunity beyond the resources one currently controls." They are referring to the unique talent of entrepreneurs to fulfill a need of, solve a problem for, or provide a benefit to a customer, even when they do not have all the required money, people, facilities, or equipment readily available to do so. Despite not controlling needed resources, entrepreneurs find ways to launch new organizations or to sustain existing ones.

A story about three people on a plane trip demonstrates the entrepreneur's penchant for recognizing and pursuing opportunity. A venture capitalist sat next to the window, an entrepreneur occupied the middle seat, and a Hell's Angel biker hulked in the aisle seat. A fly buzzed around and landed on the lapel of the venture capitalist, who brushed it off; it landed on the lapel of the entrepreneur, who brushed it off; and then it landed on the chain-and-leather vest of the biker, who grabbed it and ate it! Moments later, another fly buzzed around, again landing on the lapel of the venture capitalist, who brushed it off; and again landing on the lapel of the entrepreneur. This time, the entrepreneur grabbed it, turned to the biker, and said, "Do you want to buy a fly?" That entrepreneur recognized and pursued opportunity!

Entrepreneurs often pursue opportunity in niche markets by developing some competitive advantage that gives them an edge in serving a targeted set of customers. Many emerging enterprises try to compete on the basis of price and specifications. But in an increasingly competitive environment, these alone are usually not sufficient for success. Entrepreneurs, therefore, emphasize intangible qualities that can be powerful in persuading customers to buy. These include attributes such as quality, ease of use, reliability, productivity, convenience, and other qualitative factors that add value or utility to a product or service. For example, rather than focus on the eldercare market, Joseph Sansone homed in on a niche in home health care for children and created Pediatric Services of America. Beti Ward developed American International Cargo, an air and ground cargo transportation service, by focusing on an underserved niche market in perishable, unusual, and oversized freight items.

Opportunity can spring from recognizing the unique in the familiar. This explains why most entrepreneurs start businesses in a field in which they have some experience by coming up with a different twist or new approach to providing products and services to others. Marguerite Sallee, confronted with child-care hassles as a working mother, created Corporate Family Solutions. This onsite child-care provider for employers allows parents to check on their children during lunch and work breaks. Joe Mitchell quit his job at a telecommunications company to start his own firm in the same industry, VarTec Telecom, because he saw an opportunity to use independent sales agents—value-added resellers—to expand telecom services.

Relating the Unrelated

Entrepreneurs also seize opportunity through "bisociation"—a phenomenon historian Arthur Koestler observed in the creative process in his book *The Act of Creation*. Bisociation is the ability to relate two seemingly unrelated concepts—to take two wildly different things and to put them together in a new way. The result of combining what appears to be uncombinable is to produce that "ah-ha" sensation in the marketplace.

Michael Dell combined computers and mail order to launch Dell Computer Corporation; Fred Smith related mail and overnight delivery to start Federal Express; Jim McCann matched flowers with a phone number to build 1-800-FLOWERS; Steven Jobs and Steven Wosniak used a fruit to name a computer company and called it Apple; Pleasant Rowland mixed doll-making with American history to form The Pleasant Company; Jeff Bezos put a bookstore on the World Wide Web to create Amazon.com. These creative and surprising combinations can be extremely effective ways for entrepreneurs to gain share of mind as well as share of market.

Koestler in his book tells the story of the rancher who's visiting with a farmer. Their conversation soon turns to the size of the property that each owns. The rancher asks the farmer to tell him how big his farm is. The farmer points and says, "Well, if you go from the edge of my house, over to the oak tree, then cut across to that creek, then go up the hill to the stone wall, then come around to that big rock over there, then circle over to the barn and then back to the edge of my house, that's my farm." The rancher, looking rather proud, says, "Well, on my ranch, I can get in my car at dawn, travel all day long, and at nightfall, I'm still not at the other end of my property." To which, the farmer replied, "You know, I used to own a car like that!" The farmer was making a bisociative connection between cars and property.

I recall explaining this concept of bisociation to Brad Armstrong, an attorney turned entrepreneur, a few years ago as he was starting a moving company in Austin, Texas. To generate his own bisociative thinking, he began to relate a range of images to his enterprise. He wanted something that had a positive feeling, was big (since he intended to grow the company), and would, as he said, "Stick in the customer's mind." After trying a variety of concepts, testing them with customers and developing prototype designs, he decided on calling his company Blue Whale Moving. On the side of each of his trucks is a huge blue whale. It's impossible for someone seeing his trucks on the highways of the Southwest not to remember the company. The surprising image helped him gain share of mind, not just share of market, since Blue Whale Moving became one of the fastest growing moving companies in the region.

By exploiting a niche, capitalizing on the unique in the familiar, and especially by thinking bisociatively, entrepreneurs demonstrate over and over an almost magical ability to recognize and pursue opportunity. In that pursuit lies the challenge, reward, and vitality of the entrepreneurial process.

9

Ready, Fire, Aim

Effective entrepreneurs are dreamers who do. I like this depiction of the entrepreneur because it combines the ability to envision the possible with the chutzpah to make it happen. After all, it's one thing to have passion, purpose, and opportunity; it's another to do something about them. This is where the entrepreneur's proclivity for action plays such an important part in turning dreams into realities. "Ready, fire, aim" is a common approach to making decisions, solving problems, and taking advantage of opportunities.

Imagine that you are in the following situation. You are walking up a timbered mountainside with a group of other people. Suddenly and unexpectedly, a huge firestorm erupts in the forest and begins to sweep uphill toward you. The flames are solid and 100 yards deep. An inferno engulfs the entire side of the mountain below you. The heat is so intense that whole trees explode into burning torches in an instant. You and the others turn and begin to run up the steep mountainside. It is a race for your lives—reaching the crest of the mountain means safety. But the fire is faster than you are. You know that you cannot outrun the fire, that you cannot reach the top of the mountain before the fire reaches you. What do you do?

Guts and Logic

This situation actually happened. In his profound and deeply moving book, *Young Men and Fire*, Norman MacLean recounts the great Mann Gulch fire of August 1949. Sixteen smoke jumpers from the U.S. Forest Service were trapped on the side of a mountain when the blowup occurred. As they started their race for life, Wag Dodge, the head of the crew, did something remarkable; he invented an escape fire—he actually started his own fire in the face of the inferno, lay down in the burnt-out area, and then let the firestorm roar over him. He was proactive in the extreme. He tried to get the others to join him, but each refused and continued running up the hill, all but two to their deaths. Dodge acted to change the situation rather than let the situation dictate his response. That's what entrepreneurs do.

MacLean makes an important observation about Dodge's invention. He points out that, "Like a lot of inventions, it could be crazy and consume the inventor. His invention, taking as much guts as logic, suffered the immediate fate of many other inventors—it was thought to be crazy by those who first saw it." Nevertheless, Dodge had the logic to see the validity of the escape fire concept and the guts to commit to it. While Dodge invented the notion that he could burn a hole in the fire, MacLean poetically maintains, "his biggest invention was not to burn a hole in the fire but to lie down in it. Perhaps all he could patent about his invention was the courage to lie down in his fire."

David Stassen's flagship product—a spinal implant to treat chronic back pain—was initially thought to be crazy. But after years of proselytizing, making presentations, and finally gaining FDA approval, surgeons rushed to order the devices immediately after they were available, and Spine-Tech became a quarter-billion-dollar company.

Joanna Lau, like other "turnaround" entrepreneurs, took over a troubled company. By reshaping its strategy, remobilizing its employees, and renewing its customer base, she turned Lau Technologies from a failing military contractor into a multimillion-dollar diversified technology firm.

Proclivity for Action

Entrepreneurship is essentially a practice that ultimately depends on performance. Entrepreneurs who perform demonstrate Steven Covey's first habit of highly effective people—to be proactive. Proactivity, according to Covey, in his *7 Habits of Highly Effective People*, means that our behavior is a function of our decisions, not our conditions. We have the initiative and responsibility to make things happen. Reactive people are driven by their circumstances; they make excuses about what prevents them from doing something.

I'm reminded of the story of the boy who came home with five "F's" and a "D" on his report card, showed it to his father, and asked, "Well, Dad, is it the genes or the environment?" Proactive people, on the other hand, are "response-able." Rather than let a situation determine how they would act, proactive people act to change their situation.

Ed Iacobucci faced the classic David–Goliath situation. His company, Citrix, which he founded in 1989, pioneered revolutionary "thin client" computing that allows PCs and devices to access software applications from a central server, over wire or through the air, without concern for bandwidth. When Microsoft announced it would develop its own thin-frame software and thus enter Citrix's market, Citrix's stock collapsed, losing 60 percent of its value in one day, February 26, 1997. Iacobucci negotiated nonstop with Microsoft representatives from February 27 to April 12, exploring any possible deal. He finally won a five-year co-development agreement for $75 million with possible software commissions of up to $100 million. In a sense, he burned a hole in the fire that was about to engulf his company. His proactivity not only saved Citrix but put it on another growth trajectory.

Consider this proclivity for action in the greatest play in my opinion in all of more than thirty Super Bowls. After all else is forgotten about these games, one play from the 1993 game between the Buffalo Bills and the Dallas Cowboys will remain in my memory with the clarity that only comes from the combination of surprise and insight.

Late in the game, Don Beebe of the Buffalo Bills proved to the claim that one person can make a difference, that one individual, by not accepting his environment as given, can even change the course of history.

In the midst of a hopeless situation for his team, Beebe performed. Leon Lett of the Dallas Cowboys had recovered a fumble, had run 60 yards and was about to score. Then Beebe appeared as if out of nowhere, having run nearly the length of the field, knocked the ball out of Lett's hand, and demonstrated that inches and instants can matter, even in lost causes. In that moment before Lett was to cross the goal line, Beebe altered a bit of history. No touchdown, no greatest score in Super Bowl history, no inevitability to this apparently inevitable event.

Beebe's 10 other teammates on the field, many of whom were closer to Lett at the start of the play, had conceded the touchdown. But Beebe chose not to. He acted to change the situation, just as effective entrepreneurs do time and again.

This bias for action—this determination not to accept one's environment as given—is the defining approach to how successful entrepreneurs pursue opportunity.

10

Being Boss

Why would anyone choose the life of an entrepreneur? Why would anyone consciously want to work long hours for low pay; give up the security (perceived or real) of employment in government, a large corporation, or even a university; willingly walk the tightrope of success and failure; and tolerate constant ambiguity by wondering where the next investment will come from or how to make payroll?

We sometimes look at a successful entrepreneur, and his or her rise to the top appears to be so easy. Jennifer Lawton founded, built, and then sold her multimillion-dollar Net Daemons, Inc, a networking computer solutions company. She was stunned by the impression of an employee who wanted to emulate her:

I was alarmed when one of my employees wanted to run a soft-ware company we were spinning off. At first, I thought that was great. When I interviewed her for it, I said, "Now I just want to let you know what goes into this." I laid out the scenario of my day and how I had to do 500 different things and that it takes 20 hours a day. She said, "Well, you know, I was going to have an assistant and do 20 hours a week." It just blew my mind that her knowing me, knowing my kids, and knowing my whole life, that she still had this concept that it was that easy.

The Real Reason

Many aspiring entrepreneurs have this same impression. I'm reminded of the aspiring entrepreneur who asked a very successful entrepreneur about how much work was involved in starting and building an enterprise. The successful entrepreneur said, "Well, the bad news is that you have to work seven days a week." "Oh," replied the entrepreneur wannabe, "that's an awful lot of time." "Yes," said the successful entrepreneur, "but the good news is that you only have to work half a day." "Oh," said the budding entrepreneur, "that's great!" "Now," said the successful entrepreneur, "you can choose to work the first 12 hours or the second 12!"

So whether it's 12 or 20 hours a day, what's the real reason that people do it?

One might assume that the primary motive that people become entrepreneurs is to make a lot of money, that they start companies to become rich. Certainly, people don't want to lose money, and they hope that their enterprises will be profitable.

But the pursuit of money or the desire for great wealth is not what drives most to undertake the process of starting and building an enterprise.

Most who choose the entrepreneurial route do so for a very different reason—one more basic, one more self-fulfilling. They want to be their own boss. The desire to control one's own destiny is a much more compelling and widespread motive behind entrepreneurial behavior than the accumulation of riches.

Research on entrepreneurs reveals their overwhelming need to control and direct. They want to be in charge—of their companies, of their decisions, of their performance. In other words, they start companies to gain more control over their own lives. With this control comes independence and perhaps wealth. If riches result, then that's an outcome of their choice of walking to the beat of a different drummer. If riches don't result, then they still may have a lifestyle that lets them do their own thing.

Internal Locus of Control

Entrepreneurs, thus, demonstrate a strong internal locus of control. That is, they believe in their ability to control the environment through their actions and therefore are willing to assume the risks entailed in starting a business. They prefer not to answer to someone else, to set their own work schedules, to make their own mistakes. Because they are internally rather than externally directed, successful entrepreneurs take personal responsibility for their success, and perform best in situations where they have personal responsibility for results.

In their book, *Seeds of Success*, William Walstad and Marilyn Kourilsky report on national surveys of youth and the general public and find that this same pattern holds. Over 40 percent of high school students and over 50 percent of the general public who wanted to start a business indicated that their major motivation was "to be my own boss." Only 21 percent of youth and 14 percent of adults thought that "earning lots of money" was the primary reason that they would want to become an entrepreneur.

In fact, seven in ten youth and nearly eight in ten adults cited nonmonetary reasons for why they would like to start a company. In addition to the strong desire to control their own lives, they indicated a desire to improve something—themselves, their families, or their communities. As Walstad and Kourilsky point out, "The stereotypical equating of the desire for entrepreneurship with the desire for money gives a distorted view of the entrepreneur."

As every successful entrepreneur can testify, just having the desire to control one's own life is not enough to build a successful company. It also takes a willingness to do the 500 different things and work the 20 hours a day that Jennifer Lawton talks about. But consider the possible rewards of being your own boss—having the freedom to do what you want to do, being able to make and live with your own decisions, being personally responsible for your own well-being and security, being independent enough to take care of yourself and those closest to you—and you begin to know what really motivates entrepreneurs to take their entrepreneurial leaps of faith.

11

Wing Walkers

E ntrepreneurs are usually referred to as risk-takers. But I don't think this is quite accurate if we mean by that the gambler who is willing to bet everything on one role of the dice and then prays that it comes up seven or eleven.

A better analogy would be the chess player who may make a bold move but also understands the parameters of the game and anticipates the possible countermoves. In the powerful movie *Searching for Bobby Fischer*, a chess master instructs his young prodigy: "Don't move until you see it!" He is telling his student not to move a piece until he sees the repercussions of his actions and anticipates the possible countermoves on the outcome of the game. At one point in the film, the teacher sweeps his arm across the board scattering the chess pieces on the floor to force the boy to concentrate on envisioning what is likely to happen, and implores him again: "Don't move until you see it."

I've never met a successful entrepreneur who wakes up in the morning, rubs his hands together, and gleefully exclaims, "How much risk can I take today!" There are times when entrepreneurs must "bet the company." But they never do so willingly, and they take this action only when no other alternative is apparent.

Richard Schulze faced a do-or-die situation when his Sound of Music stores were being pushed out of business by larger competitors. So he scrapped his old business, applied and embellished the superstore strategy that was being used against him, changed product offerings and advertising approach, and created Best Buy. "If it hadn't worked," he said, "clearly it would have sunk the company. Without the money from selling all these products, I couldn't pay our bills, and it would be all over."

Minimizing Risk

Every effective entrepreneur seeks to minimize risk—by using other people's money, by demonstrating market acceptance of an innovation, by developing a working prototype of a product or technology, by securing orders before manufacturing, by getting paid before delivery.

The entrepreneur's approach to risk involves both guts and logic. But what one sees usually depends on where one is standing. The entrepreneur tends to see the logic of the risk while the person observing the entrepreneur tends to see only the guts.

To minimize risk, the entrepreneur prefers the odds to be stacked in his or her favor. Importantly, the entrepreneur seeks to secure those odds by acquiring superior knowledge about the domain in which the risk is taking place. The more the entrepreneur knows about the risk, the more calculated it becomes.

Consequently, the entrepreneur tends to see the logic rather than the guts of the risk.

Scott Cook developed a working prototype of Quicken so he could show there was no technological uncertainty. Michael Dell got customers to pay for computer products before he made them so that he had a steady revenue stream. David Stassen created market acceptance for his spinal implant device before it was approved by the FDA so as to ensure customer demand. Marc Beige secured orders from large retailers for his costume company before manufacturing the costumes.

Calculated Risk

Rather than freeze with indecision in the face of unexpected developments, entrepreneurs are willing to take calculated risks because they know something about the environment in which they are operating and have come to terms with the possible ramifications of the risk. Entrepreneurs thus feel able to deal with the probability of failure—that is, the riskiness—of the situation.

This is different from the monk who had labored many years at his monastery. One day a torrential rain began to fall, and the river began to rise. A rescue boat came by and told the monk to get in and be taken to safety. But the monk replied, "No, the Lord has provided in the past, and He will provide now." The rain continued until the river had risen to the steps of the monastery. A second rescue boat came by, but again the monk refused to go, saying, "No, the Lord has provided in the past, and He will provide again." Finally, the river rose so high that the monk had to flee to the highest steeple of the monastery. This time a helicopter came by and lowered a rope ladder. But the monk rejected the offer a third time, saying, "No, the Lord has provided in the past, and He will provide now." The rain continued, and the monk drowned. When the monk approached the gates of heaven and met St. Peter, he was upset and angry. "Why didn't the Lord provide?" he yelled at St. Peter, to which St. Peter replied, "What do you want? We sent two boats and a helicopter!"

The person on the outside of the entrepreneurial process tends to see the guts rather than the logic of the risk. To the person on the outside, the entrepreneur can appear to be taking an enormous gamble, to be making a leap of faith into uncharted territory. Because the person on the outside doesn't understand the calculated nature of the entrepreneur's decisions, the entrepreneur can appear to be crazy. This is especially so when someone gives up a good-paying job to start his or her own company. Some were probably surprised when Jim Koch quit his $250,000 per year consulting job to start his Boston Beer Company. But his family had been in the beer business, so he had a good idea of what he was getting into. The view of risk from the outside is often why it is so hard to get investors to fund new ventures, and why so many may look at a startup venture and predict that it will never succeed.

To hedge their bets, entrepreneurs try to follow the code of wing walkers, those daring souls who venture out to the tips of airplane wings: "Never let go of one thing until you have a hold of something else." They try to manipulate an aspect of the risk that gives them some control in an ambiguous situation. This is the basis of the explosion of home-based entrepreneurs who start a company at home on nights and weekends while still holding onto their 9-to-5 jobs.

The perception of risk associated with starting and building a company is at the very heart of what entrepreneurship is about because it reflects the entrepreneur's ability to manage elements of, and thus feel more comfortable about, the unknown.

12

Creating Credibility

Launching a new company brings up a hidden challenge that I find few entrepreneurs are even aware of, much less know how to deal with. Consumed with the search for capital, the recruitment of talent, and the development of the product, the emerging entrepreneur often doesn't consider the first question on the mind of a prospective customer: "Who the heck are you!?"

When customers wonder—"Who is this person? Why should I buy anything from this company? How do I know these folks can deliver?"—they are really trying to decide whether you are credible.

Credibility is at the heart of any business relationship. The ability to inspire belief in oneself and one's company separates really successful entrepreneurs from those who never quite reach their potential. All of us want to work with someone in whom we have confidence, someone whom we feel will not let us down.

Credibility is especially critical for the emerging entrepreneur about whom the customer may know little or nothing. So how can an entrepreneur develop credibility?

Regis McKenna, the Silicon Valley marketing guru, provides an essential insight into building credibility in his book, *The Regis Touch*. He points out that there are three ways to build credibility—through inference, reference, and evidence.

Credibility Through Inference

Even without personally knowing an individual, we can assume or infer credibility if we are aware of key accomplishments in his or her past. A good resume can go a long way in impressing others. An entrepreneur can build credibility through inference by pointing to facts, experiences, and credentials that allow customers to judge him or her as a competent, informed, and knowledgeable individual.

Elements in the entrepreneur that suggest or infer credibility include:

- *Academic credentials and degrees.* Expertise in a discipline, as shown through levels of education, conveys knowledge about a subject. That knowledge is a basic building block to demonstrate understanding about the activities in which one is engaged.
- *Previous successful experience as an executive, manager, or entrepreneur.* Been-there, done-that experience is a powerful way to communicate that one can do it again. This type of background

reinforces the view that a person actually knows what he or she is doing, since he or she has done it before.

▌ *A track record of directing completed projects.* Having been involved in a key project, whether that be developing a product, assisting in a marketing campaign, or overseeing the finances of an initiative, shows that one has demonstrated a skill that can be applied to other projects.

▌ *Ownership of patents.* Showing that one has applied for and received patents is another way to indicate the ability to accomplish things. Especially for technologically innovative companies, this can reinforce the perception of having technological know-how.

Credibility Through Reference

A second, and higher, level of credibility is reference. This is what others say about you and your company. This is part of the personal trail that we all leave behind us as we go through life. Those who provide references on you may be others in the company, opinion leaders in your industry, media sources who write about you and what you produce, and customers and suppliers with whom you have interacted. References may take the form of conversations that are part of a due diligence process; articles in newspapers, trade journals and magazines; testimonials from customers who have used your product or service; and awards and recognitions that you and your company may have received.

The more objective the reference, the more believable the impact. I once interviewed a woman for a key position in a startup company. At the bottom of the resume, I noticed that one of her references was a person who had the same last name as she did. I asked who the person was and found out it was her husband. When I asked her why she thought he could be a good reference, she replied that he could be totally objective and unbiased about her. I just didn't believe that. I told her that the last thing one should want in a spouse was someone who was totally objective and unbiased. But that is what someone should look for in an effective reference that builds credibility.

Imagine that your company is a movie and you are the star— what would the critics say that you could use as endorsements to promote your enterprise and to encourage others to trust you?

Credibility Through Evidence

The next, and highest, level of credibility is evidence. Evidence includes the quantifiable facts of success—increasing revenues, additional product offerings, expanded market growth, higher stock valuations, expanding quarterly earnings—whatever demonstrates that the company is a thriving enterprise. This clearly takes time to develop. But these proofs can powerfully demonstrate the viability of an enterprise and the credibility of the person who leads it.

Through inference, reference, and evidence, entrepreneurs enhance and expand their credibility with customers, suppliers, bankers, investors, and the general public. As they do, something remarkable happens—they gain share of mind and not just share of market.

13

Tolerating Strength

In surveys of high-growth entrepreneurs, it emerges as their number-one issue—the challenge to recruit and retain talent. Perhaps no other issue is as critical to the ongoing growth and vitality of an organization as the ability to attract and keep really outstanding people.

Some may think that recruitment is simply a matter of job posting or using a headhunting firm or tapping online resume services, and that retaining employees is simply a matter of providing benefits like health insurance or 401(k)s or paid holidays. But in the fast-growth firm, recruiting and retaining talent is the most critical responsibility of the entrepreneur.

Every entrepreneur must develop or acquire the know-how and expertise to run an expanding enterprise. This involves the practical but essential ability to manage change both personally and organizationally. Personal know-how involves skills such as leading, communicating, listening, and negotiating. Organizational know-how involves marketing, finance, accounting, production, and manufacturing.

As companies grow, successful entrepreneurs learn that they cannot do everything themselves. Consequently, they must find ways to bring in others who complement and extend their own skills or who make up for gaps in their own knowledge and experience. Bob Bernstein, co-founder of Bernstein–Rein Advertising, now a $300 million a year firm that has had major accounts with clients such as Blockbuster, McDonald's, and Wal-Mart, learned that lesson early on in the growth of his company. During the startup phase, he paid talented people more money than he was making (though he did not tell them that) to get the expertise that he needed in the firm. By minimizing his own compensation so that he could pay others more, he got the talent that he needed to grow the company. He believed that with the right people he could make his company more valuable and that that would eventually be better for him. Other successful entrepreneurs think the same way, and thus actively pursue creative ways to recruit and retain talent.

Marilyn Kourilsky at the Kauffman Center for Entrepreneurial Leadership points out in her research that what emerges as the entrepreneurial team usually has an extremely strong affinity for the entrepreneur and a commitment to the integrity of the entrepreneur's business vision. This team, if given the freedom to act, engages in entrepreneurially innovative and proactive applications of its group skills to scale up the venture's resources, processes, and performance.

Letting Go and Holding On

For the entrepreneur, bringing in talent requires something much more significant than the ability to find complementary skills or additional expertise. It demands that one learn to tolerate strength in others. Peter Drucker has observed that effective leaders are "not afraid of *strength* in their associates. They glory in it." For me, therein lies the crux of successful or failed team building. Ironically, there is a paradox at work here. The entrepreneur must confront his or her fear of letting go, of being out of complete control. So the practical issue for the entrepreneur is to learn how to let go, which requires trusting others to take responsible and informed action.

Successful entrepreneurs will hold on to the vision, values, and culture of their companies while letting go of many of the operating functions to other more experienced, talented individuals. That's what Kay Hammer has done. Her company, Evolutionary Technologies International in Austin, Texas, provides sophisticated data management tools to clients in banking, health care, insurance, and other industries. As the company has grown to over $30 million in annual revenues and 170 employees, so has its need for executive talent. "As we grew, we hit a level of complexity where the people who had been our managers could no longer do the job," she says. "They could not scale up with our growth. The three senior managers I have on board now joined us knowing how to take us to the next level. Every morning when I come in and see them, I breathe a sigh of relief." She maintains, "If I had made the decision to bring in outsiders sooner, our company's bottom line would be better off."

One of the most telling examples of tolerating strength in others is Michael Dell, the wunderkind turned corporate leader of *Fortune* 500 company Dell Computer Corporation. He has shown time and again the ability to hold on to the vision, values, and culture of Dell Computer while bringing in and working with extremely strong individuals. The result has been stunning growth, making Dell one of the most dramatic success stories of the 1990s.

Early on in the growth of the company, which at that time was called PCs Unlimited, Dell met Lee Walker. Walker was in his late 40s while Michael was in his early 20s. Walker, a gangly 6 ' 9 " Harvard MBA with extensive entrepreneurial experience running his own growth companies as well as being an executive in other larger firms, had agreed to have dinner with Dell to discuss bringing in a president to the growing firm. The two hit it off, and Dell convinced Walker to join the firm, providing not only an attractive stock option package but, just as important, the authority and responsibility to run the firm as president. Dell, as CEO and chairman, remained in charge of the direction and strategy for the firm. The two made the classic dynamic duo, leading Dell through its initial public offering, one of its most chaotic and fastest growth periods.

Dell showed the same willingness to tolerate strength by structuring a vocal, experienced, and demanding board of directors, including George Kozmetsky who had co-founded Teledyne Corporation and helped to start several others, and Bobby Ray Inman, who had held key positions in Washington and a *Fortune* 500 company.

The adage is to "hire someone smarter than you," but an entrepreneur's ego can often make that easier said than done.

Two Key Attributes

Tolerating strength in others requires of the entrepreneur two key attributes—one mental, the other practical. The first is a willingness to look for and celebrate the uniqueness and diversity of others, to value and reward the performance of others, and to be confident enough in oneself not to fear the accomplishments of others. Thus, Pierre Omidyar brought Meg Whitman in as president of eBay; Ed Iacabucci recruited Mark Templeton as president of Citrix; and Jerry Yang and David Filo made Tim Koogle CEO and president of Yahoo!

The second attribute is a determination to do whatever is necessary to get the right person into the company at the right time. This may require offering stock and other performance incentives, understanding and addressing special personal needs (like helping to find a position for the spouse or making arrangements for the sale and purchase of houses), providing unique insurance benefits, addressing title and status within the firm, structuring unique work and vacation arrangements, and delineating clear lines of authority and responsibility.

For the entrepreneur who can mentally and practically tolerate strength in others, the reward can be a thriving and increasingly valuable company.

14

The FUD Factor

Ralph Waldo Emerson, the great nineteenth-century American writer, has led many an entrepreneur astray with his famous phrase: "If you build a better mousetrap, the world will beat a path to your door." Therein lies many a disillusioned entrepreneur and failed company. Entrepreneurs who sit and wait for the customers to come to them wind up sitting and waiting while the world passes them by. The only entrepreneurs who succeed are those who beat a path to the world.

Smart entrepreneurs know something about human psychology and appreciate the hesitation that customers can feel when dealing with a new company or considering the purchase of an innovative product or service. Consequently, to help customers understand the benefits of their products or services, entrepreneurs must first learn and respect the customers' state of mind.

If they do, they can take an approach to dealing with customers that is neither technical nor fancy. It just works!

Successful entrepreneurs use FUD to their advantage. FUD stands for Fear, Uncertainty, and Doubt. Most customers tend to have a high degree of FUD when considering whether to do business with a new or emerging company about which they may know little or nothing. The more innovative and costly the product or service, and the less well known the entrepreneur or the company, the higher the degree of FUD in the mind of the customer.

Reduce FUD

Consequently, entrepreneurs face two choices. The first is to reduce FUD in the minds of customers. They do this in a variety of ways:

- *Do the customer's homework for him or her.* Research the company's needs to understand the customer's issues and challenges even better than he or she does. Gain insights into topics such as the company's competition, competitive advantage, and purchase decision process before you talk with the company.
- *Justify to the customer the cost of the product or service.* This may require that you prepare a cost–benefit analysis, and that you justify the substitution cost of replacing what they are currently using with your product or service.
- *Encourage project teams.* Try to get employees in the company to participate with you in defining the problem to be solved,

clarifying needs, and testing the product or service. This can be critical in helping customers gain a sense of ownership in adopting the produce or service.

▌ *Stress the benefits of the product or service rather than its features*—that is, how it helps the customer rather than what it does. Show how the product or service meets a customer need or solves a problem rather than describing how the product or service operates.

▌ *Provide support.* Reinforce a purchase decision by providing guarantees, warranties, or training.

▌ *Demonstrate.* Actually show the product or service to remove any questions that it actually does what you say it will do. The ability to prove a product, visualize a value, and illustrate intangibles is a powerful way to reduce FUD.

Increase FUD

The second choice is to increase FUD in the mind of the customer so as to persuade him or her to buy. That is, entrepreneurs alert customers to the negative consequences of not using their products or services. They do this in a number of ways:

▌ *Indicate that the customer will fall behind the competition.*
This requires understanding what competitors are doing, and showing the customer how your product or service can actually enhance his or her competitive position.

▌ *Show that the customer's operation will be less efficient.*
This requires insight into the customer's distribution, manufacturing, or marketing and selling processes, and

demonstrating how your product or service can streamline those processes.

▌ *Provide data that productivity will decline.* This requires showing how your product or service is actually a productivity tool for employees to maximize their abilities to get the work done.

Parable of the Stethoscope

A few years ago, I worked with a startup company that developed an electronic stethoscope. The device had remarkable abilities to pick up the sounds of the internal workings of the body and provided superior technical improvement over the traditional rubber acoustical stethoscope. By listening with this device, physicians could pick up the incredible cacophony created by the different sounds of the various organs of the body.

The entrepreneur who held the patent on this device began to advertise it in the *Journal of the American Medical Association* (JAMA), a leading publication in the medical field. The ads emphasized the nature of the frequency wave in the new stethoscope compared with the more traditional kind and showed a picture of two waves—one going up (the entrepreneur's) and one going down (the traditional one). At the bottom was an order form. The entrepreneur did not get a single order! He was emphasizing a feature rather than a benefit of his innovation, and few buy features.

I encouraged him to understand the knot in the stomach of physicians—what worries them and keeps them awake at night. One major concern is malpractice. So the entrepreneur began to reduce FUD by stressing the benefits of his product—that it improved diagnosis, had been fully tested in medical schools, and came with a money-back guarantee. He also increased FUD—by indicating that incorrect diagnosis led to malpractice suits. The result was that sales began to go up.

Fun, Usefulness, and Delight

The modern variation of Emerson's phrase is, "If you build it, they will come." They never do!

Consequently, entrepreneurs in emerging companies must be attuned to the worries, issues, and perceptions of customers and aware of the power of FUD in the mind of the customer. By developing products and services that meet real needs and solve real problems, they can overcome the Fear, Uncertainty, and Doubt that customers may have. By appreciating the very real concerns that customers feel, they can choose approaches to increase or decrease FUD to effectively persuade customers to see the Fun, Usefulness, and Delight of their products and services.

15

PROFILE:
The Consummate
Entrepreneur

O f all the entrepreneurs I have known and worked with, one stands out as the consummate entrepreneur. That was Ewing Marion Kauffman. I've often reflected on Mr. K, as he was known, and our interaction during the year and a half before his death in August 1993.

For me, he represents the consummate entrepreneur not because of what he built, but because of how he built it.

His is the classic entrepreneurial success story. After World War II, he was a salesman for a pharmaceutical company working strictly on commission. He could sell, and he loved selling pharmaceuticals. When he made more money than the president of the company, the president cut his commission and took away part of his territory. So he quit. He started Marion Laboratories in the basement of his house in Kansas City with a $5,000 investment and the sole desire to take care of his family. He called the company Marion instead of Kauffman Laboratories so his customers would not realize it was just a one-man operation. He prepared and packaged pills and injectibles at night, and sold them to physicians during the day.

I asked him once if he thought he was taking a risk by giving up a well-paying job to launch his own venture. "No, Ray," he said, "You see I went to my three best customers and asked them if they would continue to buy from me if I could supply the same quality products at the same price. Because we had such good relationships, each said yes."

People said yes a lot to Mr. K as he built Marion Laboratories from that one-man, home-based business with $36,000 in revenues in 1950 to an international, pharmaceutical corporation with 3,400 associates and $1 billion in annual revenues in the 1980s.

He never used the term *employee*. Everyone who worked at Marion was an "associate." "I don't want to work for someone, but I do want to work with someone," he explained to me.

He merged Marion with Merrell Dow in 1989 and sold the merged company to Dow for an estimated $6.5 billion. Not bad for a poor kid from rural Missouri, whose mother daily reminded him growing up, "Ewing, others may have more than you, but no one is better than you."

As the company grew over those four decades, so did he. He recruited people who were better than him in different aspects of the business, developed and implemented policies and procedures at every stage of his company's growth, and clarified and solidified his own and his company's values and beliefs.

The remarkable financial success of Marion is not what makes Mr. K the consummate entrepreneur to me. What I find myself reflecting on time and again is the way he put principles into practice.

He insisted that you treat others as you would like to be treated. He knew firsthand the disappointment, personal and financial, that can happen to people when they are taken advantage of or mistreated, as he felt he had been working as a salesman for that other pharmaceutical company. He determined not to let that happen at Marion. He argued that treating others as you want to be treated was not a religious sentiment, but simply the right way to behave and the best way to make money. This sentiment required that one assume the good in others, and thus approach them with dignity, respect, and honesty.

He advised, "This is a tough one to live up to, but trust everybody that works with you. There will be many times when you are taken advantage of, but in the long run, you will be further ahead, company-wise, profit-wise, and certainly you will be happier." There were legendary stories about new associates to Marion who would strike deals with vendors and suppliers that served Marion's interests while putting others at a disadvantage. Mr. K would ask them how they would feel if they were the vendor or supplier, and then send them back to negotiate a true win–win arrangement. The relationships this engendered served Marion well during hard times in the 1970s.

He believed that those who produced should share in the rewards. A pleasant-sounding sentiment, but one that carried a demanding requirement for those at Marion. He made it clear that if you did not perform, you could not stay in the company since you were not honoring your responsibilities to the others in the organization. So he shared equity with associates in the firm who performed—a rather revolutionary idea in the 1960s and 1970s. The result was an incredibly motivated, dedicated, and high-performing workforce that felt genuine ownership in and pride from their work. On the day of the merger with Merrell Dow in 1989, over 300 associates became millionaires, and many others accumulated significant wealth because Mr. K encouraged them to be entrepreneurial enough to bet on their own performance.

Mr. K also believed in giving back. He was convinced that those who succeeded had an obligation to return something to the community and society that made their success possible. So he bought the expansion Kansas City Royals baseball team in 1966 when no one else came forward to do so, even though he had no previous interest in baseball. He believed that his town could not be a big league city without a big league team.

He trained tens of thousands of people during the 1970s in CPR using the field of the baseball stadium after one of his associates nearly died of a heart attack on the warehouse floor. He created programs in the 1980s for kids at risk to help them get through high school, avoid drugs, and build self-esteem. And, after selling his company, he committed himself and his wealth to establish the Ewing Marion Kauffman Foundation to advance his two passions—promoting youth development and accelerating entrepreneurship in America.

He experienced joy in giving. "The greatest satisfaction I have had personally is helping others, doing something that either inspires them or aids them to develop themselves."

Today, Marion Laboratories is gone. But something more important lives on—the legacy of a consummate entrepreneur.

The spirit of this legacy is best exemplified in the credo that Ewing Kauffman and his associates wrote for Marion Laboratories, which they called Foundations for an Uncommon Company. They wrote, believed in, and lived the following:

> *We have the responsibility for excellence and innovation. We do all that we do to the very best of our ability and with the strongest enthusiasm we can generate. It is the very nature of our business to do things that have never been done before and for which there are always reasons they cannot be done. Success for us requires the ability and spirit to find a pathway through any obstacle, even when no pathway is visible at the start.*

Therein lies the pathway to success for every entrepreneur.

Section III

SKILLS OF ENTREPRENEURS

16

Luck and Networks

Whenever successful entrepreneurs recount the launch and growth of their companies, they will invariably at some point mention how lucky they were. Lucky to have found the initial key customer, lucky to have raised critical financing at a crucial point in the company's development, lucky to have hired the right people at the right time, lucky to have attracted key board members and advisors, just lucky to have gotten some help from some source at the pivotal time that they needed it.

Certainly the fortuitous occurs, and an accidental discovery can come at a propitious time in a company's growth. Serendipity can strike the entrepreneur, as it can anyone, and he or she can come across something valuable without even consciously looking for it. Chance can play a role in the entrepreneurial process. But something deeper is also at work.

Network Builders

In a significant way, entrepreneurs make their own luck. The adage is that "the harder one works, the luckier one gets." But work at what? Rather than toiling away all alone in pursuit of their ventures, successful entrepreneurs work at building and using networks. These networks play an essential role in enhancing an entrepreneur's luck.

Howard Aldrich, a professor of sociology at the University of North Carolina–Chapel Hill, has shown through his groundbreaking research the important connection between networks and entrepreneurship. Entrepreneurship is facilitated or constrained by linkages between entrepreneurs, resources, and opportunities and by the social relationships through which entrepreneurs obtain information, resources, and social support. Thus, entrepreneurship is embedded in networks of continuing social relations. Successful entrepreneurs, in other words, are effective network builders.

The more extensive, complex, and diverse the web of relationships, the more the entrepreneur is likely to have access to opportunities, the greater the chance of solving problems expeditiously, and ultimately the greater the chance of success for the venture. Just the opposite is also true. The fewer, less dense, and more homogeneous the web of relationships, the less likely it is for the entrepreneur to succeed.

In sociological terms, successful entrepreneurs work to expand weak ties rather than strong ties. Strong ties are those that we have with those closest to us—family and friends. These relationships usually reflect similar values, backgrounds, and preferences, but they don't necessarily expand the entrepreneur's knowledge or experience base. Weak ties, on the other hand, are relationships with a much broader range of individuals. They may be linkages with acquaintances, contacts, colleagues, or associates, many of whom may have very different backgrounds, experiences, knowledge, and resources than those of the entrepreneur.

Leveraging Resources

Through networking, entrepreneurs leverage human, financial, and technological resources. By developing linkages to people who bring varying backgrounds, broader experiences, and more and different resources than the entrepreneur may have, entrepreneurs enhance their luck in finding what they need when they need it to build their ventures.

In a real sense, for the entrepreneur growing a company, it's not only what one knows but also who one knows that can make a difference in taking advantage of an opportunity, solving a problem, acquiring key information, or gaining access to a needed resource.

A story about how well an entrepreneur is networked reinforces this point. An entrepreneur is visiting with the president of the United States in the Oval Office. If the phone rings and the president takes the call, then the entrepreneur has a limited network. If the phone rings and the president tells his secretary to hold the call, then the entrepreneur has a good network. If the phone rings and it's for the entrepreneur, then that entrepreneur is well networked!

Entrepreneurs who are building companies consciously build their networks. They develop ties with professionals, like accountants, lawyers, marketing experts, and bankers. They try to get to know other entrepreneurs who have more experience than they do or develop contacts with university professors whose students may do projects for their companies. They participate in gatherings of entrepreneurs and professionals, like breakfast meetings, venture fairs, training programs, and entrepreneur associations. They call people and ask for a little time to discuss an issue or problem. When they meet people, they take time to learn about what others know and do, and then exchange business cards. They ask others for small favors—like reading and commenting on their business plan, introductions to key people, access to information, what to read about an issue, and recommendations on where to go for help. They engage others—on planes, during conferences, at receptions—about their businesses. They expand their web of relationships by building their card file. As a result, they tend to be luckier than those who remain by themselves, working alone, because they have broadened and deepened their connections to others who have access to resources, knowledge, and expertise.

So are successful entrepreneurs lucky? They will say they are. They will also make their own luck by pursuing and taking advantage of their networks with others.

17

The Most Hated Skill

It causes sweaty palms, nauseous stomachs, and dry throats. It seems complicated and burdensome, even unnatural. It comes easy to few. Most business schools relegate it to a kind of lowly vocational training; many don't teach it at all. If a company's very survival did not depend on it, most entrepreneurs would ignore it. But successful entrepreneurs say it is essential that anyone who wants to build a viable enterprise must learn to do it. Anyone who wants to succeed as an entrepreneur must sell.

Ken Meyers, who built Smartfood into a multimillion-dollar healthy snack food business, captured the sentiment of many entrepreneurs when he declared, "There is nothing in this world that I hate more than selling!"

Selling All the Time

Selling is the most hated skill to many entrepreneurs because it smacks of hucksterism, of arm twisting, of getting people to buy something they neither want nor need. It's tinged with falsehood, misinformation, and deception. It reflects a kind of Willy Lomanism drudgery. Finding prospects, qualifying them, making presentations, negotiating over price and specifications, and especially closing a deal—asking for the sale—is a daunting and sometimes intimidating process for many entrepreneurs.

But selling doesn't have to be that way. For successful entrepreneurs, selling takes on a positive, proactive, and even creative aura. It provides continual opportunities to understand real customer needs, to be responsive to changes in the market and to create value. It is a form of communication, in fact, that can give entrepreneurs immediate feedback on what they are doing right or what they should be doing differently. That's why successful entrepreneurs are selling all the time. Ken Meyers observed:

> I had to sell every day all day, to everyone I encountered, from my parents to let me keep borrowing money to buy my boxes of rice in the old days, to my distributors, who were complaining about one thing or another, to the retailers who wanted more money or wanted to kick us out, to my employees who without constant coddling and selling would quickly lose motivation and lose faith and morale.

Mastering the Skill

Three ways of thinking not only help entrepreneurs become comfortable with the concept of selling but even eventually allow them to master the skill of selling.

First, entrepreneurs sell themselves before anything else. That is, they sell what they stand for and the values that are important to them. Jim McCann, who made 1-800-FLOWERS a national success and who is a master salesman, observed, "You have to have a set of core values and beliefs so your banker, your employees, your customers all know that these are your values, and you hold them precious and you'll do whatever you have to do to make things happen in a good and positive sense. But you won't compromise those values." What we think about ourselves affects how we interact with others.

Second, entrepreneurs sell what they love. Believing in the value and benefit of a product or service is a fortifying requirement in overcoming the initial fear of somebody saying no, in rebounding from the rejection that is sure to occur, and in persevering in the face of people's objections. Entrepreneurs who are good at selling are usually providing something that they think is worthwhile in some way. When no one walked into her first store to buy her chocolate chip cookies, Debbi Fields took a tray of them outside and nearly begged people to try them. She wasn't just selling a cookie; she was selling something that she was proud of. She was selling a delicious way for people to feel good for a little while. How we feel about what we do influences how others perceive what we do.

Third, entrepreneurs build relationships. Selling for successful entrepreneurs is not just about initiating a transaction. It's about making and keeping a promise to a customer. By listening, asking questions, and probing, entrepreneurs come to understand what customers genuinely need and want, and then they provide that to them. James Stowers founded American Century with a $2,000 stake and then built it into a $100 billion investment firm not by trying to get people to buy mutual funds but by helping them achieve financial independence. What we call what we do makes a significant difference in how we think about what we do.

Every entrepreneur brings his or her own unique talents, knowledge, and experience to an entrepreneurial venture. But all, in one way or another, sell. They sell themselves, their concepts, their business plans, their products or services, even their hopes and dreams to others. The more entrepreneurs learn how to sell and the better they get at it, the more this most hated of skills becomes the most practiced of contributions to entrepreneurial success.

18

The Three Universal
Laws of Marketing

I buy books from Amazon.com. It is convenient, fast, easy, and secure. I click in, make my selections, and click out. I do not worry about giving my credit card number; I believe the books will be delivered quickly; and I know that the company will follow up with me to make sure it got my order right. Along the way, I realize that Amazon.com follows my three universal laws of entrepreneurial marketing.

Law 1: It is more important to be significantly different than a little bit better.
So often I see companies trying to outdo competitors by being a little bit better rather than by being significantly different. They try to add a little bit more memory to their chip or make the monitor a little bit bigger or run their programs a little bit faster.

But this is a game that emerging firms can't win. Competitors can simply augment their memories, enhance their monitors, and speed up their programs. It's the same with other kinds of products and services. The secret to success in the market is to be really different; to set yourself apart from competitors by clearly and consistently differentiating what you do.

Entrepreneurs make their companies significantly different by:

▎*Understanding the environment of their customers.* By this I don't mean the socioeconomic environment that surrounds us. I mean the internal, working environment of individuals. Savvy entrepreneurs work to understand the knot in the stomach of their customers. They learn what their customers worry about, what keeps them awake at night, and thus what prevents them from purchasing. Knowing this, entrepreneurs can then position their products and services to address and eliminate these concerns, and thus encourage customers to buy their products and services.

Amazon.com, for example, ensures confidentiality in the purchase process. So I don't have to worry about using my credit card. The software company, Ashton-Tate, called its first product dBASE II, even though it was the first version, because George Tate realized that no one wants to buy the first of anything. And a medical device company that I worked with focused on the issue of minimizing malpractice suits for doctors rather than the technical aspects of their product.

▌*Focusing on intangibles.* Too many entrepreneurs think they can succeed by competing on price or specifications alone. They can't. Don't get me wrong. Price and the specs of a product are important. But by themselves they don't differentiate effectively enough. As surely as the sun rises in the east and sets in the west, if an entrepreneur competes only on the basis of providing a cheaper product or a faster machine, someone will come along and provide the same thing at a lower price or a faster pace. Intangibles on the other hand—like convenience, reliability, quality, upgradability, service, and ease of use—provide powerful incentives to buy. Amazon.com makes it easy and convenient for me to buy, so I do. eBay provides a sense of community among its users, even calling groups "neighborhoods."

▌*Targeting customers.* No product is bought by everyone. Therefore, entrepreneurs must target a specific group of customers and then meet their needs. If one is developing software for doctors or architects, then which kind of doctors or architects? Danny O'Neill has a fast-growth coffee company in Kansas City. His gourmet, "air-roasted" coffee is designed for more elegant restaurants and the coffee aficionado. Sam Walton started Wal-Mart by targeting smaller, rural communities that the then big retailers believed to be unprofitable.

By being significantly different, companies make themselves unique in the mind of the customer. And gaining share of mind is the way to gaining share of market.

Law 2: Customers don't just buy a product or service. They buy trust.

Successful companies are trusted by their customers. Trust is the basis of loyalty; it's the foundation upon which companies not only survive but also thrive. Trust is hard to achieve, must be proven day-in and day-out, and is easy to lose. To gain the trust of customers, entrepreneurs:

- *Keep promises.* Entrepreneurs continually tell customers that they will do things for them. They often don't realize that when they indicate what they will do, they are making promises. When a company tells a customer that his or her order will be there the next day, that's a promise! When Federal Express launched its now famous advertising campaign to deliver packages "absolutely, positively overnight," it made a promise. Because it delivered on that promise, customers truly trusted that their packages would be there absolutely, positively the next day. Smart entrepreneurs know that they don't let their mouths or their ad campaigns or their promotions made a promise that they or their companies can't deliver on.
- *Build credibility.* A company's reputation is its most treasured asset. Reputation—good or bad—is a reflection of how everyone in the company interacts with the customer. It's based on the credentials of the entrepreneur and the management team, the values that employees demonstrate, and the evidence of success, like the visibility and growth of the company. By their action or inaction, companies create impressions, engender testimonials, and leave reference trails.

One sign of credibility is the good word-of-mouth that comes from satisfied customers. Just as people talk about the latest movie they've seen, they talk about the good and bad experiences that they have with companies. For example, I like purchasing books on Amazon.com, so I tell others about my positive experience. The opposite is also true. In fact, research indicates that those with a good experience with a company will tell three others, whereas those with a bad experience will tell ten others.

▎*Fix mistakes fast.* Most customers realize that companies, like people, aren't perfect, and that mistakes will happen. Smart entrepreneurs know that fixing mistakes fast is essential to retaining trust. I buy a lot of flowers from 1-800-FLOWERS. The people who answer the phone are cordial and helpful; the flowers that get delivered are beautiful; and the service is reliable. But the company did make an error on one of my orders. When I called to let the company know, the agent immediately apologized, refunded my money, and gave me a discount on my next order. I can live with that.

A company gains the trust of its customers by being trustworthy. And being worthy of trust means treating the customer as the entrepreneur who heads the company would want to be treated.

Law 3: A complete product is the totality of what a customer buys.
Whenever I buy books from Amazon.com or flowers from 1-800-FLOWERS, I'm not buying just books or flowers. I'm buying

an experience. I'm buying a Web site that's easy to navigate, a simple purchasing process, confidentiality and security when I use my credit card, cordial and helpful people on the other end of the phone when I call, and an ability to fix mistakes fast and without question.

Too often, entrepreneurs think that customers just want a specific product or service, and they forget all the other expectations that customers have along with the product or service. Entrepreneurs who are attuned to the range of customer expectations surround their products and services with all the support, features, acts, and information that add not only real value and utility but also comfort for their customers.

Like Newton's laws that govern the physical universe or the periodic table that delineates the elements of nature, these three laws, from my experience, govern the marketing universe and delineate the elements that move products and services into the marketplace. Companies that understand and follow these laws will move forward, making discoveries and solidifying their competitive advantages. They will have satisfied customers who keep coming back again and again, clamoring for more. Those that don't will wind up like those inventors trying to build a perpetual motion machine or those alchemists trying to make gold out of lead—frustrated and defeated—because they keep trying to defy the laws of the universe.

19

Leaders and Laggards

One of my favorite cartoons depicts the problems that entrepreneurs encounter in introducing products into the marketplace. It shows a king on horseback with his arm raised above his head, brandishing a sword, about to lead his troops into battle. A fellow is standing next to him with his foot upon a machine gun. The caption has the king saying, "I can't be bothered seeing a crazy salesman. I've got a battle to fight!"

The Wrong Customer

Although the fellow's innovation could radically change the nature of the fight, either for the king or his adversary, the king doesn't realize it, and the salesman isn't doing anything to change the king's point of view. Worse, he doesn't realize that he's trying to sell his innovation to the wrong customer.

This happens a lot in the business world. Entrepreneurs spend a lot of time and effort trying to get new products into the marketplace and never understand that they're talking to the wrong customers. Rather than try to figure out who the right customers are, they usually approach any possible customer, and thus often meet people with the same attitude as the king on his horse.

The king has no interest in trying a new product. He loves his sword; he is comfortable with his sword. He was trained on that sword; his father and grandfather used a sword; even his adversary uses a sword. This sword has won him many battles in the past. So why should he change? Why should he try something that's foreign to him, that will cost more money than his sword, that he's not sure will perform as well as his sword, and that requires a whole new learning curve to implement? Besides, he doesn't have time to try this innovation. He's about to go into battle. Later is better, when he's not so pressed for time.

So what's an entrepreneur to do?

Diffusion of Innovation

In situations like this, go with theory because the theory is powerful. To my mind, the most important discovery related to marketing new products and services is the theory of the diffusion of innovation. The theory postulates that in any given social milieu, such as a country, state, city, community, church, school, company, or market, people are spread across a bell-shaped curve in terms of their attitude toward innovation. They range from those who are wild for any innovation to those who have to be dragged, kicking and screaming, like the king, to anything new. The spread across the curve has the following distribution:

- *Innovators.* On the left of the curve, making up 2.5 percent of any given population, are the innovators. These are individuals who love the newest bells and whistles and will try anything simply because it's new. This is not the most important group for entrepreneurs to focus on because they don't relate their interest to any practical use or application.

- *Early adopters.* As you move to the right on the curve, 13.5 percent are early adopters. This is the critical group for entrepreneurs to identify and work with. They like trying new things because they want something that performs tasks better. More important, these people are opinion leaders. They are the consultants, industry luminaries, business experts, company groundbreakers, trade journal writers, and media and Wall Street analysts who are constantly looking for the new new thing that will enhance performance. As opinion leaders, they can accelerate the introduction of a new product into a marketplace because they influence others to buy. Whom do they influence?

- *Early/late majorities.* The largest segment of a population, like a market, is the early and late majorities. Each composes 34 percent of the people in that population. The early and late majorities look to the early adopters to help them determine whether or not to buy a new product or service.

▌ Laggards. These are people like the king on the horse. They
simply want nothing to do with the latest-greatest, whatever
it might be. These folks believe that the computer is a passing
fad, and the typewriter is about to make a comeback!

Accelerating the Diffusion Process

Entrepreneurs should focus on identifying and working with the
early adopters in their markets so as to speed the introduction of
new products to customers. To find early adopters, ask others in
your industry to name who likes to try new things; find out which
companies have a track record of serving as a beta site or test
center for new products; keep your own list of customers who seem
willing to experiment; make a list of luminaries, trade journal
writers, consultants, and media people who write about developments in your business area; monitor who attends trade shows;
and ask others, like advisors, who are knowledgeable about your
industry to identify people and companies that have developed a
reputation for being innovative.

Once you've identified early adopters, you can be more proactive than the fellow standing next to the king. To help with the diffusion process and to bring your product to the attention of early
adopters do the following:

▌ *Show product advantages/benefits.* One of the most effective ways
to do this is to demonstrate the product. The fellow next to the
king, for example, could fire the gun! In other words, show how
what you have will improve performance for the customer.

▌ *Emphasize compatibility with lifestyles/workstyles.* Every new product is a substitution for an older one, one that people may have become comfortable with because it has come to fit their lifestyles or workstyles. Thus, show how the new product can enhance lifestyle and workstyle, that is, how it might make things easier, faster, or more effective.

▌ *Reduce reluctance to change.* Offer warranties, guarantees, and money-back assurances to encourage people to try the product.

▌ *Communicate failure consequences.* Let the customer know what will happen if he or she chooses not to use the innovation. For example, the king would have to face the possibility that his adversary may have the advantage of the product while he may not.

Winning the War

The theory of the diffusion of innovation has a powerful and practical message for every entrepreneur who wants to introduce an innovative product or service into the marketplace. Don't knock on just any customer's door. Don't get stuck with the laggards. Identify and seek out the early adopters—those opinion leaders who influence others to buy. If you do, you're likely to win, not just the battle, but also the war.

20
Orchestra Conductor

A successful entrepreneur is like the conductor of an orchestra. He or she brings together skilled musicians, emphasizes how each instrument must work with and complement the others, and then transforms initially discordant sounds into a harmonious symphony. To get the best out of the group, the entrepreneur must blend a wide variety of talents while giving the most gifted performers the opportunity and the stage to excel. The result is that the members of the orchestra may not only create beautiful music, but may also share a feeling of pride in being part of something larger than themselves.

Dr. Tom Velez, who not only holds a Ph.D. in math but also is a gifted violinist, knows firsthand the connection between conducting and leading a company. He used the connection to build CTA, a space and communication information technology company, into a

$200 million enterprise. As a scholarship recipient at The Julliard School of Music in New York, he said that he "had the opportunity to study orchestral conducting, a fabulous experience that would serve me well as a future CEO." He recognized that musicians play their instruments better than the conductor, just as many in a company have better technical skills than the entrepreneur. The role of the great conductor, like that of the successful entrepreneur, is to integrate a broad spectrum of skills and personalities by allowing for personal expression while insisting on organizational excellence.

Power of Great Groups

Leadership scholars Warren Bennis and Patricia Ward Biederman in their insightful book, *Organizing Genius*, talk about the power of great groups. They point out that great groups don't just happen. They are made and become coordinated teams of original thinkers. The first step is for leaders to be unafraid of hiring people better than themselves. They thus focus on two key elements in the recruitment process: excellence and the ability to work with others. When these two elements are present, great groups can become extraordinarily productive, but only when everyone in them has the opportunity to be entrepreneurial. Scott Cook, who founded Intuit, has recognized this as his company has grown:

> *A lot of companies that start entrepreneurial don't wind up that way. I think what happens is that often companies may end up feeling entrepreneurial for the founder or CEO, but may not*

feel entrepreneurial for anyone else. A truly entrepreneurial company has to feel entrepreneurial for all the people who are in the company.

When a company feels entrepreneurial for all the people who are in it, the entrepreneur is effectively orchestrating talent. But how can we determine whether an entrepreneur has the ability to orchestrate talent?

The Ability to Orchestrate Talent

There are some telltale signs: an ability to assemble diverse teams of people; a knack for working with and through others; a capacity to add value without being totally in charge; a talent to coach and develop others without taking over for them; a willingness to share the credit.

Scott Kriens has built Juniper Networks into one of the fastest growing and most successful technology companies on the Web by orchestrating talent. The company, with over $100 million in revenues and more than 350 people in 1999, develops backbone routers and unique software to enhance infrastructure systems on the Internet. The company's technology enables Web service providers to meet the demands of an expanding Internet. Kriens recruits for three key qualifications: a passion for learning, a commitment to excellence, and a love of technology. People thus come to Juniper Networks to work with an extremely gifted talent pool. And they bring in others. Kriens has instituted a company-wide program in which every employee is chartered with bringing in a new employee. The company has also established its "top ten most wanted list" for additional talent, and employees who recruit people for one of these positions are rewarded with a trip. By having everyone help build the talent pool of the company, Kriens has created an environment that encourages personal expression while requiring organizational excellence.

Just as the conductor recognizes the excellence of the violinist in the first chair, the entrepreneur who leads a great group finds ways and times to subsume his or her ego to the egos of other talented people to ensure that the company feels entrepreneurial for everyone who performs.

21

Quick and Cheap

Entrepreneurs are exceptional learners. They learn from everything. They learn from customers, suppliers, and competitors. They learn from employees and associates. They learn from other entrepreneurs. They learn from experience. They learn by doing. They learn from what works and, more important, from what doesn't work.

In the process, they find out what they are good at. I'm reminded of the story of the boy who took his ball and bat in the backyard to practice his hitting. He told himself that he would be the greatest hitter of all time, tossed the ball in the air, swung, and missed. He picked the ball up, told himself that he would have a longer hitting streak than Joe DiMaggio, tossed the ball in the air, swung, and missed again. He picked the ball up one more time, told himself that he would hit more homeruns than

Mark McGwire and Sammy Sosa combined, tossed the ball in the air, swung, and missed a third time. Then, he picked up the ball, thought for a moment and exclaimed, "Wow, what a pitcher!"

Learners Rather Than Knowers

Every entrepreneur must find out what he or she is really good at, and then apply that learning to running an enterprise. This involves the practical but essential ability to manage change both personally and organizationally. Pat Cloherty, a leading venture capitalist, emphasized the importance of learning this way: "Running a business is not an emotional aspiration. Running a business is a substantive skill, and, in its finest form, it is artistic. . . . [Entrepreneurs] have to have the skills associated with running a business in a detailed fashion."

Entrepreneurs who develop great companies in the next century will hone their business building skills if they accelerate learning, first (and especially) for themselves and then for everyone else in their firms. Jim Collins, co-author of *Built to Last*, argues that those who build exceptional companies must become learners rather than knowers by "responding to every situation with learning in mind." This can be done by setting explicit learning objectives, developing a "to-learn" list, replacing performance goals with learning goals, and setting time aside "to discuss or reflect on events and extract the maximum knowledge and understanding from them."

Cathy Hughes, who has built a successful chain of radio stations along the East Coast, responded with learning in mind when she saw the opportunity to launch her company:

> *The first thing I did was study the FCC manual. The basics start with what are the rules, and the FCC is the regulatory agency that sets the rules. How are you going to play this game if you don't even know what the rules are? That's where I started and became virtually an expert on how the FCC operates.*

Everyone Learns

This learning approach then must extend to everyone in the organization, as Jack Stack has done at Springfield ReManufacturing Corporation, which started deeply in debt, now does over $120 million in annual revenues, and has spun off 26 other companies. He initiated open-book management to help every employee learn to make decisions in the best interests of the company:

> *We were going to try to get them [employees] in a position to give them enough tools to be able to make entrepreneurial decisions. We were in a situation if we were going to be short $10,000; we were going to be history. If we made a $10,000 mistake, we were going to be dead. In order to be able to communicate that kind of knowledge to 119 people, we felt that the only way we could deliver the message was to begin to teach them financial statements, to virtually open up our books to them. Not only*

open the books but create a way to show that they made a difference, to try to create this flow of information, of contributions, where they began to see where they fit in terms of the financial outcomes of the company.

Entrepreneurs who embrace learning will exhibit a number of specific behaviors that can indicate whether they have the ability to learn. These include a willingness to admit when one is wrong; participation in regular mechanisms for getting good feedback; an ability to realistically appraise strengths and weaknesses; a willingness to be responsible for one's own actions; and an ability to learn from mistakes and the mistakes of others.

As one successful entrepreneur advised, "Learn to fail quickly and cheaply!" Anyone who does is likely to build a very good company.

22

Students of Human Moves

G reat entrepreneurs are students of human moves. They are constantly watching, evaluating, sensing, interacting with, responding to, and anticipating customers. Rather than seek only shares of existing markets, successful entrepreneurs are customer driven to build relationships, find new users, and develop better and expanded applications, all of which generate new market opportunities.

For example, I occasionally receive personal e-mail from Jeff Bezos, founder and CEO of Amazon.com. His electronic correspondence starts, "Dear Ray." Though I've never met "Jeff," I like this. What he's trying to do, I suspect, is establish some kind of personal tie with me, try to get me to use his service more than others, and learn what kinds of books I prefer to read so that he can tailor his service to my needs. And tailor his service he does!

Now when I go to Amazon.com, I'm greeted by name, with a suggested list of books that I might like to read based on my previous selections, with recommendations from others who have bought the kinds of books that I've purchased, and with references to newly published books that reflect my areas of interest. Jeff Bezos strikes me as a student of human moves.

Share of Mind

Because consumers have so much more power today in determining the shape and delivery of products and services, entrepreneurs must think differently about customers and take greater risk in trying to gain share of mind and not just share of market. They must build credibility rapidly, be more aggressive and innovative, and rely more on judgment and intuition. To do this, they must have an appreciation for how people behave.

My favorite example of an entrepreneur's understanding of his customers comes from Ashton-Tate, a software company, which was acquired in the early 1990s for over $400 million. George Tate's homerun product was dBASE II, one of the first database management software systems. dBASE II implies there was a dBASE I. There never was. One could argue that this was a marketing trick, a deceptive ploy. But the product did what it said it would do. And Tate knew that no one wants to buy the "first" of anything, that people believe that if they wait six months the product will cost less and work better. He was a student of human moves.

Entrepreneurs who pioneer products and services in the marketplace are not only students. They are also teachers. While they are learning from the marketplace, they are also educating it. They do more than promote. They teach. In fact, the learning is inseparable from the teaching. One constantly reinforces and expands the other.

Education is not an end. It is a process. It requires an ability to communicate appreciation for, knowledge about, and experience in a subject. By conveying benefits and values, entrepreneurs seek to instill in their customers a willingness to become personally involved with the product, as anyone who has ordered a double mocha latte from Starbucks can testify.

Being Educated by the Marketplace

Successful entrepreneurs, therefore, are constantly educating and being educated by the marketplace. Because of this, they are especially attuned to the value of complaints. Jim McCann whose 1-800-FLOWERS has established a reputation for outstanding customer service, put the education that can come from complaints this way: "If a customer complains, he can tell you what's wrong with your service, what's wrong with that person, what's wrong with the process, and you have a chance to fix it. You also have a good chance to go back to that customer and make good by him."

When a product or service solves a real problem or meets a real need, it reflects a deep appreciation for and knowledge about the customer. When the customer is educated to the product's values and benefits, the result can be the "ah-ha" sensation of discovery that comes with customer-driven products. The cash cow products, the company makers, like Quicken at Intuit, are those that spring from sensing the pulse of the customer and then matching real product differences with real customer needs.

Becoming educated to the marketplace requires quantitative information and qualitative insights. One springs from data, the other from experience. One relies on numbers, the other on judgment. One demands objectivity, the other personal involvement.

Great product campaigns educate largely because they use the power of demonstration. Potential buyers become vicariously or directly involved in understanding what the product can do for them. From sampling the newest flavor at the ice cream shop to trying out the latest technologically innovative golf club for 30 days on a no-risk, satisfaction-guaranteed basis, entrepreneurs find ways for customers to decide what they want. The ability to prove a product, show a benefit, visualize a value, illustrate intangibles, or display differences is an entrepreneur's best teaching tool. It's the best not only because it reduces uncertainty but, more important, because if it reflects an understanding of human moves, it also captures the imagination.

23

Napkins and Plans

The back-of-the-napkin approach to business planning has a storied place in the mythology of entrepreneurship. The venturing journey starts something like this. Over dinner, two promising entrepreneurs start talking about ideas for launching a company. During the salad course, they brainstorm a range of concepts. Through the entree, they narrow the opportunities down and begin talking about raising money. By the time dessert rolls around, they've latched onto a great concept, determined the marketing strategy, and tabulated the cash they need to start and grow the enterprise. But now they need to put all this down on paper. So they grab a napkin, turn it over, and sketch out their business plan. The next day, they show the back-of-the-napkin plan to a venture capitalist who immediately writes a check for what they need, and the two entrepreneurs are off on their entrepreneurial odyssey.

Doing and Planning

Starting companies on the backs of napkins may have happened occasionally in the past, but like the unicorn, that approach to planning exists only in the imagination of entrepreneurs today. Bankers, venture capitalists, and private investors want to see a detailed, written business plan. They want an interesting and concise executive summary, an in-depth description of the product or service, an extensive market assessment and competitive analysis, a well-defined marketing strategy, resumes of the management team, a thoughtful risk analysis, a detailed cash flow statement and three-to-five-year financial projections, and any other supporting information to help convince them that this company can succeed. They want to know that the entrepreneur has personally written the plan (rather than hire that out to someone else), completely understands what can be a complicated process, and can effectively answer questions about any aspect of the document.

Entrepreneurs, on the other hand, just want to get started. Given their unshakable belief in the viability of their concepts and their proclivity for action, most entrepreneurs dread the thought of writing a business plan. Why put so much time and effort into a document that will probably be outdated as soon as it's written? Why waste time and energy on passively putting ideas down on paper, when so many other, more important things—like making a product and selling it to customers—need to be done? Why bother with a written business plan? Why not just use the back of a napkin?

I know how hard it is to write a good business plan. I've taught business plan writing to students in graduate schools and to entrepreneurs already in the marketplace. I've read hundreds of them over the years, and I've written a number myself. Putting ideas down on paper, conducting research, organizing material, wrestling with seemingly countless questions and issues, running spreadsheets, and revising over and over again to hone a compelling document strike most entrepreneurs as a laborious and daunting undertaking. Running one's own business is the fun part of being an entrepreneur; writing about it is not.

The great American essayist, E. B. White, captured the difference between doing and planning when he observed, "Every day I wake up determined both to change the world and have one hell of a good time. Sometimes, that makes planning a little difficult."

So why should an entrepreneur write a business plan? Because it can significantly enhance his or her chance of success!

A survey of Entrepreneur Of The Year winners conducted by the Kauffman Center for Entrepreneurial Leadership found that 79 percent of these successful firms had a written business plan, whereas 21 percent did not. Further research showed that having a written business plan improved financial performance. Firms having a written business plan possessed a 50 percent greater sales growth and a 12 percent larger gross profit margin than firms not having a plan!

Benefits of a Plan

I think I know why this difference occurs. A written business plan serves an entrepreneur in three critical ways. First, it provides a sanity check. Going through the process of thoroughly assessing what could go right and what could go wrong—of putting one's idea to a true realty test—helps an entrepreneur determine if his or her idea is a genuine market opportunity. Sometimes, one learns that what seemed like a good idea at one time is really not a viable opportunity after all. The result is that an entrepreneur can save himself or herself not only a lot of money but also a lot of heartache. On the other hand, rigorous analytical thinking can reinforce the entrepreneur's belief that the concept is in fact a great market opportunity, and thus allow the entrepreneur to proceed with both additional facts and confidence.

Second, a good business plan is an effective fundraising enticement for prospective investors. It can alleviate fears that the entrepreneur does not know the market, minimize risk by showing how the entrepreneur will deal with competition, and remove doubts that the entrepreneur can run the enterprise. As a result, bankers, private investors, and venture capitalists can feel more secure knowing that the entrepreneur not only has enthusiasm for the enterprise but also business savvy.

Third, a written business plan is a useful planning tool. It can provide direction and strategy to a venture by clearly identifying where the company should go and how it should get there. As that great American philosopher of the twentieth century, Yogi Berra, said, "You got to be very careful if you don't know where you're going, because you might not get there."

For entrepreneurs to wind up where they want to go on their own epic entrepreneurial journeys, they need a map by which to travel. There will be detours, obstacles, and unexpected events along the way that will require the entrepreneur to be flexible and adaptable. But the journey will be easier and the destination will come more quickly into sight if the entrepreneur relies on a compelling business plan rather than a sketch on the back of a napkin.

24

The Entrepreneur's Rosetta Stone

E verywhere I look, there's advice on how to write a business plan. Detailed outlines, lengthy checklists, and completed example plans provide a plethora of information on what to include in a document, how to include it, and where to include it. Courses offer hands-on assistance in assembling a plan, and consultants will even write the plan for an entrepreneur.

But I see little insight into how to read a business plan.

A business plan to a savvy investor is like the Rosetta stone to an Egyptologist or a roadcut to a geologist or an X-ray to a surgeon. Just as an Egyptologist discovers the keys to ancient inscriptions by deciphering the stone, and the geologist recognizes the story of earth's development in the layers of rock in a roadcut, and the surgeon learns precisely where to operate by interpreting the X-ray, so

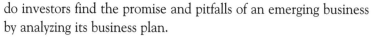

do investors find the promise and pitfalls of an emerging business by analyzing its business plan.

But what should one look for? What are the critical clues that might reveal what a business is really all about and what future it actually might have? What kinds of discoveries might actually crack the code of a proposed business and help determine whether it's a viable enterprise?

Having taught business plan writing and having read hundreds of plans over the years, I've learned what helps to separate reality from hype, at least for me, in an entrepreneur's Rosetta stone. When I read a business plan, I look to find the answers to three questions. Is there really an opportunity here? Can these people pull it off? Will the cash flow?

Is There an Opportunity?

When deciphering a plan, I go to the marketing section first. This area of the plan should reveal whether there is a genuine opportunity with the business or merely an idea disguised as a company. A true opportunity is customer driven. It addresses a real problem or fulfills a real need. Thus, I search for evidence of the following:

> ▌ *Knot in the stomach.* A convincing plan effectively describes the knot in the stomach of buyers. It delineates what buyers are worried about and why they are concerned about it. It shows, through personal experience, survey data, statistics, and buyer testimonials, what keeps customers awake at night. For example, I was impressed with a plan that offered a new

software package to expedite the approval process for Underwriter Laboratory certification on electronic devices. The plan detailed the rejection rate for first-time certification, outlined the costs for multiple applications, expressed the frustration of those applying for certification, and provided data on the lengthy time required to get certified. Clearly, there was a need here.

| *Profile of the customer.* A good plan provides a detailed profile of the primary customer. Too many plans assume that anyone or everyone will buy the product or service. A convincing plan clearly identifies who the primary buyer is and why that person is the primary buyer. I read a plan that offered a new kind of drawing material to artists. But not just any artists. The plan focused on commercial artists, described their likes and dislikes, delineated how they worked and where they purchased art supplies, and identified their key artistic issues. I believed the entrepreneurs behind this plan really knew their customers.

| *Direct interaction with customers.* A winning plan shows direct interaction with the possible purchasers of the product or service. By involving customers in product development, using beta sites, conducting in-depth surveys, generating purchase orders, directing focus groups, and demonstrating one-on-one contact with real customers, a plan can communicate personal connection to real customers. For example, a plan for a company selling salsas and other sauces provided the results of detailed taste tests that convincingly showed customer delight with the products.

Can They Pull It Off?

If the plan lays out a real opportunity, I assess the people who are presenting it. I try to determine whether the entrepreneur and the team have the competence, commitment, and passion to turn the opportunity into a viable enterprise. So, I'll search for clues on the following:

- *Talent.* What kind of know-how and experience do the entrepreneur and the team bring to the venture? Since I'm trying to determine their credibility in the written document, I'll look for evidence like previous success in other ventures or projects, credentials in their areas of expertise, ownership of intellectual property, and knowledge of the industry in which they want to compete. The general partner of a venture fund that I know decided to pursue a poorly written plan because the two individuals who wrote it were highly regarded scientists, owned a number of patents on their technology, and had worked for several years in the industry in which they wanted to compete.
- *Skin in the game.* It's awfully easy to spend someone else's money. Consequently, I look to see whether the entrepreneurs have invested any of their own money in the venture. Putting some of their own money into the business indicates a level of commitment that shows genuine seriousness in the venture. I see a lot of business plans today written by graduate students who want to start companies. Many indicate that they can't put money into their ventures because they don't have any to put in. I always encourage them to find a way to put something into it. The amount of money is less important

than the fact the entrepreneurs are willing to invest more in their venture than their own sweat equity.

I *Passion.* Although passion cannot be quantified, I do believe that it can be communicated in a plan. I want to bet on someone who has the energy, enthusiasm, and zeal to pursue what to that person is a worthy, challenging, and uplifting purpose. Consequently, I look at how entrepreneurs tell their story to understand why this business is an important endeavor and to sense what really motives the founders. I read a plan from one entrepreneur who was downsized, set up a business in his basement, and then through persistence and hard work discovered that it could grow. That fellow had passion for what he was doing.

Will the Cash Flow?

Finally, I assess whether the entrepreneur knows enough of financials to effectively evaluate the cash flow position of the company. Projections of revenues are too often misleading. They always project success. In fact, in my experience, all projections are "conservative," no matter how incredibly optimistic they may be.

More telling than projections is the cash flow statement of the company. If the entrepreneur can accurately and completely tally actual expenses and income in detail, then the plan presents a realistic perspective on critical milestones and on whether and for how long the company can stay above water until an infusion of capital is necessary.

Deciphering a business plan requires a bit of detective work. Analyzing information, detecting clues, and interpreting findings are all part of determining the viability of a venture. Even after that, there is no guarantee of success for the business. But by looking for the right signs, the mystery of identifying truly promising enterprises may become clearer.

Opportunity, committed people, and cash flow—those are the keys that crack the code of an entrepreneur's Rosetta stone.

25

The Powerful Pitch

A few years ago, *The Book of Lists* identified the fourteen worst fears of people. Number six was death. The number-one fear of people was talking before a group. People were more afraid of public speaking than of death!

I can empathize with that. I watch entrepreneurs give presentations on their companies to prospective investors. So many of them seem to wish they were dead rather than have to get up and pitch their companies. Throats become parched, voices quaver, hands shake, knees knock. They're just not very comfortable standing in front of a group. At venture fairs that I attend, entrepreneurs often have only a few minutes to make their best cases for their companies as investment opportunities. At one fair, entrepreneurs had seven minutes. A green light signaled "start"; a yellow light indicated "two minutes"; and a red light meant "stop!"

Most of their presentations were disasters. As speakers, most of the entrepreneurs looked incompetent, and they never managed to communicate the most important points about their enterprises. It doesn't have to be this way.

Anticipating the Performance

Savvy presenters anticipate what will happen before, during, and after their presentations. They take a few practical actions that help get them ready for their performance because, in a real sense, speaking before a group is like a performance.

- *Envision the performance.* Like actors going on stage, find out ahead of time how the stage will be set up, where you will stand, how the audience will be arranged. Then review in your mind's eye every aspect of what you will do once you get on stage. Try to get to the site of the presentation early, stand at the podium, and walk across the room. By the time you give your presentation, you will have been through it already a number of times in your mind so that once you start, the scene will be familiar to you.
- *Minimize stage fright.* Every performer gets butterflies, or at least the good ones do. Butterflies in the stomach are an indication that adrenaline is flowing and that the body is ready to perform. So when you get the butterflies recognize this as a really positive sign—your senses are alert—just as good athletes do. To minimize the terror that may come once you stand on stage, take a deep breath to get oxygen into the

body. Rather than look over people's heads or avoid eye contact, find a friendly face in the audience that will smile back at you. This will help you to engage the audience, and engaging the audience will actually calm your nerves.

▌ *Own the room.* Before you start, make sure the room or stage is designed to meet your needs and focus attention on you and your story. Check all the audiovisual equipment to make sure it works, take coins and keys out of your pockets so no one can hear them rattling, and remove any distractions, like flip charts or sample products, that the presenter before you may have left on the stage.

Making the Presentation

A lot of entrepreneurs never get to the two critical issues that investors want to hear about: what's the opportunity and why can you pull it off? They talk instead about how their technology works or the patents that they've filed or the intricacies of how something is made. Not that these are unimportant. But in a venture presentation, especially a relatively brief one, the purpose is to get investors to follow up with you, at which time you can explore these kinds of details in much greater depth. To get investors to want to meet with you, you have to address their two most important issues.

The first is to present the opportunity:

▌ *Speak with pride.* Investors want to know how your company poses a genuine opportunity for investment. To communicate this, let your pride in the venture come through. Think of something you are proud of. For example, I like to think of my son's success in wrestling in high school. He started as a walk-on his freshman year and went 3–19. In his senior year, he won 30 matches, set a school record for reversals, and became a state qualifier in his weight class. A glow and warmth comes over you when you communicate your pride, and that helps win an audience over. Do this as you talk about your company.

▌ *Be customer driven.* A genuine opportunity solves a real need or fulfills a real desire. Show that you know your customers, that you understand their problems, and that you have a true solution for those problems. You might present testimonials, show purchase orders, describe a user survey or tell stories of how customers benefit from what you offer.

▌ *Prove your uniqueness.* Demonstrate how your product or service is different from others in the marketplace. By focusing on benefits and not features, by showing how your product or service helps customers and not simply on what it does, you emphasize the uniqueness of what you have. And the uniqueness of a product or service is the essence of marketing.

The second critical issue is to establish your credibility. To show who you are and why you can pull this venture off use the following elements:

▌ *Focus on your background, credentials, and experience.* From these, the audience can infer that you are competent and knowledgeable.

▌ *Highlight what others say about you*, especially customers through testimonials, results of beta sites, and third-party entities like trade journals and newspaper articles. From the evidence you present, the audience can deduce that the company is viable.

▌ *Show increases in sales*, revenues, employees, products, and other quantitative measures of growth. From the evidence you present, the audience can recognize that the company is poised for greater success.

The Flexible Presentation

When entrepreneurs focus on the themes of opportunity and credibility, they discuss what investors most want to hear about. Then, whether entrepreneurs have five minutes or fifty minutes for their presentations, they can reduce or expand their comments to meet any time frame if they follow a few guidelines.

▌ *Be redundant.* Repetition is saying the same thing in the same way over and over. Repetition is boring. Redundancy is saying the same thing in different ways so that an audience gets multiple perspectives on an issue. Redundancy is interesting. For example, to demonstrate customer satisfaction with a product or service, you can read a testimonial, then tell a story about a visit to a customer, then give data from a survey, then provide a report from a third-party source, then describe an incident between an employee and a customer, and so on depending on the amount of time you have.

▌ *Be persuasive.* You can enhance the persuasiveness of a presentation in a number of ways. Present new evidence, which could include new statistics, research, or information with which the audience is not acquainted. Avoid the one-sided story by discussing the cons of your product before the pros. Present the nature of the problem facing the customer, then show the solution that your company has to offer.

▌ *Manage questions.* Reward a question by pointing out its importance. Repeat a question to give yourself time to think and to make sure you understand it right. If you don't know the answer to a question, say so but indicate that you will find out.

Presentations are an essential part of the entrepreneurial process. How an entrepreneur communicates is just as important as what he or she communicates. So the next time you're asked to give a venture presentation, don't think you're approaching death's door. View it instead as an exciting chance to talk about what you know and love best—your company. If you do, you'll find it an enjoyable, and perhaps profitable, experience.

26

PROFILE:
Pilot as Entrepreneur

As an Air Force fighter pilot, Marc Moore learned about "situational awareness." He had to survive. At the stick of F4s and F16s, he had to be constantly alert to where his wingman was, to how his plane was responding to every turn and twist, and to the sequence of events on his target paths. While he meticulously prepared a flight plan for each sortie, he also came to expect the unexpected, learning to respond correctly and immediately to any situation. Being a fighter pilot can be good practice for being an entrepreneur!

After flying missions for eight years, Marc fulfilled a childhood ambition and became a stockbroker. He liked the investing business—working with money, the fast pace, the interaction of world politics and economics with clients, the daily score keeping—and he did very well at it. But he also knew that he wanted to be president of his own company and set a goal to achieve that by the time he was 36 years old.

One of his clients in a family-owned business was encountering family problems in the enterprise and decided to sell out. He asked Marc to help him. Marc helped write the business plan and helped raise the money for a new venture to buy him out. In return, he was offered a minor ownership in the company and a seat on the board. When the company failed to make progress, the president was let go, and the board asked Marc to take over as president of the firm. Marc became the pilot of Payroll Transfer Inc. three weeks after his 36th birthday.

When Marc took over as president in December 1989, the company had 12 employees and $3.5 million in annual revenues. He turned on the afterburners. By May 1990, the company had annualized revenues of $22 million and was profitable for the first time. The company was sold to a group of New York investors in 1996. When he stepped down as president and out of the company in March 1998, the firm had reached $400 million in annualized revenues with over 225 employees and sales representatives.

Payroll Transfer was an emerging company in the professional employee industry when Marc took over its leadership. The company essentially became a co-employer with its clients, which were primarily small businesses with five to fifty employees, although PTI eventually had client companies with over 1,000 employees. Before each pay period, clients would provide all payroll records, such as hours worked and overtime, to PTI. PTI would then produce the payroll and deliver it to its clients, who would then pass out the payroll checks to their employees. PTI, as part of its service, managed all payroll-related activities for its clients, such as benefits, worker compensation documentation, all appropriate withholding taxes, and Equal Employment Opportunity Commission materials, thus freeing them up to concentrate on their core businesses. Particularly for the small business owner, this was an extremely valuable service that saved them both time and money.

He built the company "one person at a time," looking for outstanding wingmen wherever he could find them. He wanted and rewarded perfect "10s"—those people who were dedicated, success-oriented, and had the best interests of the company, as well as their own, at heart. And he insisted that they hire 10s as well. He had a simple but powerful formula—his three circles—to bring strength into his company. He looked for those individuals who combined talent (the ability to do things well), enjoyment (a positive attitude about life as well as their jobs), and moneymaking capacity (the skill to make money for the company as well as themselves).

He sought to establish a culture of success and performance through his own example. He never went to work without a tie, was always approachable, and insisted on showing respect to everyone. He structured formal opportunities for managers to review operational issues, and talked often about the philosophy, values, and plans of the company in one-on-one meetings and with groups of employees. Every Tuesday from 8:30 to 9:30 A.M., without exception, he met with the top managers from each department to discuss operational issues related to clients, employees, and the growth of PTI. These sessions encouraged a free flow of information while helping each person become familiar with every aspect of the company. Every Friday for one hour without exception was another meeting of top management to focus on the philosophy (like the three circles), perception, and future plans of the firm. The powerful result was that eventually all employees were saying the same things, understanding the same issues, and believing in the same future.

He trusted others to act in the best interests of the company. Early in the company's development, he would get back to his hotel room while on business trips just to find dozens of voice messages waiting for him to decide on countless issues. "That drove me crazy." So he gave his employees the one rule his father had given to him when he was growing up: "I'll trust you not to do anything stupid; so don't do anything stupid!" And as long as anyone in the company made decisions in the best interest of the firm, he backed them completely and never criticized them, even if some of the decisions proved to be mistakes.

He interacted with customers continually. His goal was to "make each customer our friend." It was a goal he set for every one of his salespeople. He sought to personally understand each client's issues, listening to their concerns and learning their businesses. Although he was always selling (right up to the day before he left the firm), he never just sold; he built relationships. It was easy because he felt a true win-win-win in what he was doing. He was providing genuine benefits to the employees of his customers, supplying a needed service to his clients in a cost-effective and high-quality manner, and building his own firm at the same time.

There's a saying that there are old pilots and there are bold pilots, but there are no old, bold pilots. That doesn't apply to pilots who become entrepreneurs.

Marc's "retirement" from Payroll Transfers Inc. in 1998 at the age of 44 lasted 24 hours. He went on to start a wireless technology company and is now expanding another company in the educational technology industry. He's still moving at full throttle.

EXPERIENCE OF ENTREPRENEURSHIP

27

A Subversive Activity

E ntrepreneurship is a subversive activity. It upsets the status quo, disrupts accepted ways of doing things, and alters traditional patterns of behavior. It is, at heart, a change process that undermines current economic conditions by introducing something new or different into the marketplace.

The successful entrepreneur is like the general that Sun Tzu wrote about in the *Art of War* in 500 B.C., when he observed, "The business of a general is to create changes and to manipulate them to his advantage."

Creative Destruction
Because of the entrepreneur's ability to instigate change, economist Joseph Schumpeter's concept of "creative destruction" is an apt description of the subversive nature of the entrepreneurial process.

By coming up with something new, like the microprocessor, personal computer, and online bookstore, the entrepreneur destroys existing products, processes, and channels of distribution, thus disrupting the economic status quo. But in the wake of this destruction, the entrepreneur creates new market opportunities that are essential to economic growth and diversity.

Pierre Omidyar changed both the nature of Internet commerce and the concept of community when he launched eBay, the online auction site, in 1995. To help his then-fiancée, an avid Pez candy dispenser collector, find others who wanted to collect, buy, and sell Pez dispensers, Omidyar went on the Net. What he actually found was that an auction format on the World Wide Web created an engaging and powerful way for people all over the world to buy and sell goods quickly and efficiently. The result has been an online trading community of more than two million registered users and over two million daily transactions. eBay's sales in 1999 totaled $47 million. According to some estimates, the online auction market, which eBay created will be worth $19 billion by 2002.

Just as radical as the innovation of the online auction itself is the shape of the community that eBay has created. eBay users visit, chat, get to know one another, shop for each other, and go on vacation together. In a real sense, they have found a new type of electronic belonging, one that can link people with similar interests anywhere in the world. People have a new way to interact, get to know one another, and even look out for one another. Groups in the community self-police their areas of interest and even form "neighborhood watch" groups to guard against misuse and misrepresentation. By fundamentally changing the way people buy and sell things, eBay has revolutionized how person-to-person commerce is conducted and how people relate to one another.

The Prepared Mind

For the entrepreneur, creative destruction results from innovation. Peter Drucker has said, "Innovation is the specific function of entrepreneurship. . . . It is the means by which the entrepreneur either creates new wealth-producing resources or endows existing resources with enhanced potential for creating wealth." The way entrepreneurs are using the Internet is a stunning example of Drucker's view of innovation at work. Companies like E-Trade and Ameritrade have changed the way people buy and sell stock, and firms like HomeGrocer.com are altering consumers' buying patterns.

Innovation requires a prepared mind. Nobel Laureate Herb Simon argues that the most innovative individuals develop "chunks" of knowledge. These are sets of patterns and relationships that develop over time that allow one to see solutions to problems—to make connections between events and actions. This reflects the truth of Louis Pasteur's famous adage that "chance favors the prepared mind."

One can actually work to develop a prepared mind. This is what the effective entrepreneur does in assessing market need by getting customer feedback, tracking trends, synthesizing information, and monitoring the competition.

By innovating, entrepreneurs initiate change, and by building viable organizations, they manipulate that change to their advantage. As the organization grows, they get others to buy into the change and to win not just their involvement, but also their commitment to managing that change. This requires clarity of direction from the entrepreneur along with the delineation of roles and the development of reward systems for all those who join the enterprise.

Working from his home and then a storefront in Honolulu, Michael Hartley co-founded Cheap Tickets, Inc. He pioneered discount travel and in the process redefined the economic dynamics of the leisure travel industry. In 1986, he acquired a number of inter-island airline tickets as a form of payment from a client. Almost as a lark, he advertised a low-cost sale of the tickets in a local newspaper. He had such a remarkable public response to the ad that he tried to sell additional tickets and received an even more enthusiastic response. From his previous experience in the airline industry, he knew that airlines usually had unsold seats. He began to negotiate directly with them to sell those seats and pass along great savings directly to leisure travelers. He then scaled up his innovative business model and expanded to car rentals, hotel accommodations, and cruise packages. Today, Cheap Tickets is the leading global discount travel seller with over 1,000 employees and $340 million in annual revenues.

Entrepreneurs are, in fact, necessary subversives. Their penchant for change and their knack for pursuing opportunities creatively destroy existing systems and markets. But with this destruction comes remarkable vitality. By innovating, entrepreneurs launch new products and services, open new markets, and create real value that are essential for economic and social well-being.

28

On the Tightrope

We long for order in our lives; still, order eludes us. We seek clear lines of causality and predictability. But cause and effect is often uncertain, and prediction is usually effective only in hindsight.

In their provocative book, *The 500 Year Delta*, Jim Taylor and Watts Wacker focus on a profound shift from reason-based to chaos-based logic. A chaos world is a whitewater world, "in which change has arrived like a river system rushing at flood tide." Everything changes all the time, and at an accelerating rate. And the change is often marked by inconsistency, disharmony, and even contradiction. While many struggle to stay afloat in these rapids, entrepreneurs thrive in the turbulence.

Embracing Chaos

I recall taking a river-rafting ride with my two sons outside Aspen, Colorado. As we approached a low-level bridge, under which our raft could barely squeeze, the guide on board cautioned us to "always know where your head is at!"

In turbulent environments, entrepreneurs know where their heads are at, not because they manage or plan for chaos, but because they embrace it.

This ability to embrace chaos is demonstrated in a very funny film of a few years ago, *The Inlaws*, which matched an orderly, conservative, strictly-by-the-book dentist, played by Alan Arkin, with an unconventional, off-the-wall, make-it-up-as-you-go-along government agent, played by Peter Falk. The two found themselves in a life-threatening situation in which they faced a crazed South American dictator. Just before meeting the dictator, the dentist asked, "What should we do?" The agent replied, "Go with the flow." To which the dentist replied, "What flow?" One could not tolerate the chaos; the other embraced it.

Organizations can also embrace chaos, as Bill Harris, president and CEO of Intuit, explains:

> *The cultural signals are a non-hierarchical approach to management. An attempt—we don't always achieve this—to allow product groups to move in whatever direction they want; a great deal of autonomy. Frankly, a good deal of chaos. What we lack as an organization is process. What we lack is consistency. What we lack is the ability to always have everything moving forward in a straight line. Very often projects collide, people collide, but within that chaos come some tremendous ideas.*

Entrepreneurial organizations may lack process, consistency, and the ability to have everything moving forward in a straight line. That's a chaotic environment. But one that sparks creativity and innovation.

Structured Chaos

In their award-winning book, *Competing on the Edge*, Shona Brown and Kathleen Eisenhardt stress the importance of structured chaos as the most viable approach to business strategy in entrepreneurial organizations. They emphasize the "edge of chaos," a delicate balance between anarchy and order. They argue, "The edge of chaos captures the complicated, uncontrolled, unpredictable but yet adaptive . . . behavior that occurs when there is some structure but not very much."

It's often out of the chaos that the mythology of a company emerges. We face this chaos situation in my own organization. An expression has emerged that communicates this is to be expected, indeed is the norm: "Keep your knees bent and your eyes on the horizon."

Entrepreneurs who embrace chaos show a tolerance for ambiguity and a comfort in dealing with the unexpected. They demonstrate a willingness to change directions with new information and to use multiple approaches as needed for different situations. They reveal a knack for being able to juggle many balls simultaneously. And they reflect something of what Karl Wallenda, the legendary tightrope walker, felt when he said, "Being on the tightrope is living: everything else is waiting!"

29

Riding the Rollercoaster

Perhaps as good a test as any (and better than most) in trying to determine whether someone has an entrepreneurial inclination is to assess one's view toward rollercoasters.

The "best"—that is, the most terrifying, surprising, breathtaking, exhilarating, and fun—rollercoaster ride that I have ever taken was on the Rattler at Six Flags Over Texas in Dallas, Texas, a few years ago. I knew that I was committed to this ride when the padded halter that covered my shoulders and chest was lowered over my head and doubled clamped into the lock under my seat. This was the proverbial point of no return. I looked at my son who was seated on my right and realized that we were both smiling in nervous anticipation of what was to come. Then the unexpected happened.

We began to move *backwards*. I had not anticipated this at all. The rollercoaster was cranking in reverse. As we were pulled back higher and higher, our bodies fell forward against the body halter until we were nearly vertical looking almost perpendicular to the ground. We were then launched down through the covered boarding area and catapulted into the first hairpin turn. In moments, we were upside down, making 360 degree spins and being flung left to right and back again all the while seeming to gain increasing speed. We seemed to have our bearings one moment, and then lose them the next. As we reached the far end of the ride, the coaster slowed to another vertical, nearly perpendicular-to-the-ground stop that left us this time gazing into the clouds, and then rushed again at breakneck speed retracing the twisting, spinning route backwards to the boarding area. As we regained our sense of stability, my son and I shared the same comments, "Wow, what a ride! Let's do it again."

Tolerance for Ambiguity

Rollercoasters and entrepreneurial ventures have a lot in common. Both can be terrifying and exhilarating at the same time. They require that one be willing to let go but hold on, take calculated risks, and deal with the unexpected. The process is fraught with turns and twists that can leave the entrepreneur feeling as though he or she is upside down or moving backwards. Just when an entrepreneur thinks that the venture is going in the right direction, it hits a hairpin curve that swerves it into another. For those who get involved in an entrepreneurial rollercoaster of a venture, the response is often, "Wow, what a ride! Let's do it again."

Not everyone enjoys a rollercoaster. It can be too traumatic, too unpredictable. The ups and downs can be overwhelmingly disconcerting. Being thrown left and right and back again can be jarring. But entrepreneurs who tend to succeed at their ventures are like rollercoaster riders who, at the top of the first hill, throw their arms in the air, yell "Hands free!" and then take the ride as it comes.

What is it that allows an entrepreneur to go "Hands free!" in starting and building a company? What differentiates the person who may start from scratch and build something of significant value from the individual who flounders along the way? One key element is a tolerance for ambiguity.

The ability to deal with the unexpected and handle the unknown is part and parcel of the entrepreneurial process. Not knowing whether one can make payroll, or facing the loss of a primary customer, or needing to find capital for growth and survival puts physical and emotional strains on an entrepreneur. The person who needs routine, who expects assurances, who counts on guarantees is likely to find the entrepreneurial process an extremely disquieting experience.

Stories from the Edge

Every entrepreneur has his or her "stories from the edge." Fires, floods, embezzling employees, technical obsolescence, defection of key personnel, murderous price competition, aging physical plant, loss of financial backing, the bank calling the loan, and delays in product development can all push an entrepreneur to the precipice of failure and test the resolve of any entrepreneur. Even the apparently mundane, like misprints in brochures and letters, lack of details in directions, and incorrect dates and places for events can wreak havoc on a company's operation. These encounters with disaster—real and potential—cause sleepless nights and knots in the stomachs for entrepreneurs.

Dick Schulze, the CEO and chairman of Best Buy Company, knows about being on the edge. In 1981, disaster struck when a tornado hit St. Paul, Minnesota, destroying his largest and most profitable store. In response, Schulze gathered his 65 employees from his other stores and held a "Tornado Sale" in the parking lot. He attracted so many customers that he had to bring in inventory from stores untouched by the tornado. Disaster struck again in 1996. When Intel launched its Pentium chip, Best Buy was stuck with a load of obsolete PCs that Schulze had borrowed heavily to stock in anticipation of a big Christmas season. The company's stock fell to a low of $5 a share and angry shareholders clamored for Schulze's resignation in 1997, making this period the company's darkest hour. Instead of stepping aside, Schulze directed an amazing recovery, shifting the company's merchandise mix to more popular and profitable goods like software, home appliances, and office furniture. In 1998, Best Buy recorded earnings of $94.5 million, a 5,500 percent increase over 1997.

Entrepreneurs who survive brushes with calamity and form strong companies despite them demonstrate the kind of courage that Ernest Hemingway once described as "grace under pressure." Their tendency toward optimism, their proactivity, and their ability to inspire others—even in the most dire of circumstances—

helps them to tolerate the ambiguity of sudden, surprising, and sometimes staggering events.

I had an encounter with an entrepreneur who had built a successful manufacturing business. Then a flood wiped out a significant portion of his plant. It looked like the company would go under. I asked him what he did when he and his employees surveyed the disaster. He said that he told them that this was the perfect time to modernize and that the flood provided an opportunity to build an even better company! They did.

By tolerating the ambiguity of the situation, he managed to survive one of those whiplash turns in the rollercoaster ride of entrepreneurship.

30
Paradoxes

Entrepreneurs may sometimes appear to be schizophrenic, to be pulled in two opposite directions simultaneously. There's a good reason for that. They must constantly deal with the paradoxes of the entrepreneurial process.

A paradox is a set of contradictory or diametrically opposed elements, both of which are real and true, that exist side by side in the same environment at the same time. Managing these paradoxes is the unique responsibility of the entrepreneur.

Order and Chaos

In the entrepreneurial organization, order exists side by side with chaos. The very purpose of structure is to try to bring order out of chaos as a company grows. And yet too much order kills the energy and excitement of the building process. Every company needs policies and procedures as it develops; yet every company also needs to encourage independent thinking and experimentation. The former brings routine and clarification to the operations of a firm; the latter allows for creativity.

The best procedures manual that I've seen belongs to David and Tom Gardner's Motley Fool. *The Fool Rules!* sets out guidelines that give structure to the company's operations but communicates a trust in employees through a tongue-in-cheek approach and a sense of humor that reflect the culture and openness of the organization. The Forward tells employees the following:

> *Recognizing attention span limitations and demands, let it be said that this handbook cannot and does not cover every single little thing about working at The Motley Fool. For subjects not covered ("Why are there so many bald guys at this company? Could I sell photos of myself in FoolMart? Where the heck can I find more toilet paper?") just ask your supervisor, or Human Resources zenmeister. Just keep in mind that the meaning of life issue is a philosophical one and can really only be answered by you.*

The entrepreneur must hold on and yet let go. He or she must find a way to hold on to the values, purpose, and direction of the company while letting go of a multitude of operations through delegating, allocating responsibility, and letting others make decisions. Entrepreneurs like Michael Dell and Debbi Fields became the culture personas of their companies, promoting and reinforcing their firms' most basic values—like customer service and quality—while others ran various aspects of their enterprises.

Acting Alone but Involving Others

The entrepreneur must act alone but involve others. Peter Drucker has observed, "Whenever you see a successful business, someone once made a courageous decision." Yet to grow the enterprise, an entrepreneur must find ways to recruit and retain others. By sharing ownership in the company, through stock options, equity sharing, and incentive plans, the entrepreneur can convert others to his or her cause with the possibility of maximizing the value of the company for all those involved in its development. Bob Beyster started SAIC with a handful of colleagues in 1969 and now has over 40,000 committed employee-owners of a more than $5 billion enterprise.

The entrepreneur must take short-term actions while maintaining long-term vision. Every successful entrepreneur provides a compelling perspective of what his or her company can be, and yet must act daily to take innumerable, incremental steps to that desired future state. Steven Jobs famously told John Scully in recruiting him to Apple, "Do you want to sell flavored sugar water all your life, or do you want to change the world?" Dan Dye and Mark Beckloff set out "to bake the best dog biscuit the civilized world had ever known" at Three Dog Bakery. The Gardners' goal for The Motley Fool has been to "educate, amuse, and enrich." And yet each has worked daily in the trenches to get where they want to go. They must sweat the details focusing on each activity day by day, while keeping the big picture in front of them at all times.

Commit and Then De-Commit

Entrepreneurs commit quickly to a course of action and then de-commit if that course of action proves ineffective. They constantly test opportunities to determine their viability. The result is that entrepreneurs sometimes wind up with a different product or service than the one they started with. John Bello tried selling conventional cold tea drinks in a crowded and fickle beverage market and discovered that no one wanted to buy them. So he signed over his house as collateral to get a $1 million loan and reinvented his South Beach Beverage Company in Norwalk, Connecticut, by providing a line featuring herb-spiked teas and tonics. Sales soared from $2.1 million in 1996 to $67 million in 1998 under the brand name SoBe.

Entrepreneurs must practice patient urgency. This requires striking the precarious balance between getting things done now and waiting for the right time and circumstances to act. Given the entrepreneur's proclivity for action and inclination for decision making, patience is sometimes a difficult virtue to come by. But Gallo was right to "serve no wine before its time." And most successful entrepreneurs will swear by the adage that "timing is everything."

These seeming contradictions—order and chaos, letting go and holding on, short-term action and long-term vision, commitment and de-commitment, patience and urgency—infuse the entrepreneurial process. They are part and parcel of the daily experience of the entrepreneur. How an entrepreneur manages these paradoxes determines the very culture of the organization he or she leads.

31

Capital Food Chain

Entrepreneur: *Lord, I'm a struggling entrepreneur, and I'm feeling so frustrated. I have a great business plan for a great company, but I can't raise the million dollars to launch this opportunity. I've talked to so many investors, but they all say no. It seems like I've been trying to raise a million dollars for a million years!*

Voice: *Don't despair.*

Entrepreneur: *Is that you, Lord?*

Lord: *Yes, it is I, the Lord, and I want to tell you not to give up hope. Remember a million years to you is like a second to me.*

Entrepreneur: *Really, Lord, a million years is like just a second to you?*

Lord: *Yes, that's right, so keep trying.*

Entrepreneur: *Lord, if a million years is like a second to you, what's a million dollars like to you?*

Lord: *A million dollars to me is like a penny.*

Entrepreneur: *Lord, can I have just one of your pennies?*

Lord: *Yes, in a second!*

And so goes the challenge of raising capital for an entrepreneur. Perhaps no other experience in the entrepreneurial process is as time consuming and nerve-racking as raising capital. The search for money to fuel the growth of a company can seem like the quest for that pot of gold at the end of the rainbow—somewhere out there, but always elusive and out of reach.

With more money available for investment than at any other time in our country's history, why do so many entrepreneurs complain about a lack of access to capital, bemoan the difficulty of securing bank financing, and lament the meagerness of funding sources for new and emerging ventures? Venture capital firms have multiple billions of dollars under management; private, affluent individuals are estimated to have upwards of $50 billion to invest; federal and state government programs promise resources for startup and growth firms; and banks tout their loan opportunities for small businesses. Yet many entrepreneurs find the search for capital the most frustrating, deflating, and maddening aspect of business building. Why do they feel as though they are in a desert of funding resources while around them surges an ocean of dollars?

Finding Your Place in the Food Chain

Just as there is a food chain in nature, so there is a capital food chain in entrepreneurship. Most companies begin small, often with a solo entrepreneur, like a single cell. As a company, like a cell, divides and multiplies, it grows. As it grows, its appetite expands, and it requires increasing amounts of capital to sustain its growth. Most entrepreneurs, however, do not know where they are in the food chain. Consequently, either they go after sources of food (capital) that are inappropriate for the company's size and abilities, or they approach sources without understanding their motivations and expectations.

For entrepreneurs to successfully acquire the capital they need to grow, they must know two things—where they are in the food chain and the mindset behind the sources of capital wherever they are in the chain.

At the earliest stage of life, when an entrepreneur is just beginning a venture, the only source of capital that may be available may be the cash he or she can generate through their own resources. This may include money in savings accounts or life insurance policies or a second mortgage on the family home or even credit cards. As one entrepreneur told me, "I have my two major investors in my back pocket—VISA and MasterCard!"

As the company shows signs of life, the next step in the chain is often family and friends (who sometimes become former friends because companies fail). Entrepreneurs may go to parents or call on Aunt Sally and Uncle Joe, who've they've not seen in years, to find out if they want to invest. Usually, the mindset behind these sources of funding is emotional—to provide some support to one who is known and loved. Thus entrepreneurs need to appeal to the emotions of these potential investors. As one entrepreneur who secured startup capital from his mother told me, "Even if I fail, she'll still love me!"

As a company continues to expand, entrepreneurs may seek financing from a bank. They listen to commercials touting the bank's commitment to and enthusiasm for working with small businesses, and, after meeting with a banker, often come away angry and disappointed. This is because they fail to realize that good bankers don't like risk. They are not interested in taking chances or in gaining equity in the company. Their mindset is collateral—can the entrepreneur pay the loan back with interest and, if not, can the bank recoup its investment by taking ownership of the collateral put up to back the loan. If the entrepreneur does not have the ability to repay the debt and if he or she cannot provide collateral for the loan, then the bank will not provide financing for the company. Smart entrepreneurs often start with very small loans from banks to build up credibility with a banker and to demonstrate a capacity to pay off the debt, thus raising the confidence level of a banker to provide larger loan amounts.

Along the food chain are business angels. These private, affluent individuals invest their own money in promising ventures. They not only want a good financial return on their investment, but they also want the satisfaction of being involved in an exciting and worthwhile new venture. Their mindset is thus a combination of financial and "psychic" income. In approaching business angels, entrepreneurs thus need to show an ability to generate a good monetary return and to provide a meaningful, personal involvement of some kind for the investor.

Realistic Expectations

Since private investors, like venture capitalists, usually expect some type of equity stake in the company, an entrepreneur must have a realistic expectation of what he or she is willing to give up for what he or she is willing to receive. I once worked with an entrepreneur who had created an impressive graphics software package. He was looking for $250,000 to complete work on the technology and begin initial marketing efforts to take the company to the next stage of development. When I asked him what he would be willing to give up to secure a quarter of a million dollars for his early stage venture, he said, "1 percent." When I told him no investor would view this as a reasonable deal, he opted to move ahead alone, and the company ultimately went out of business for lack of funds. He, like a lot of entrepreneurs who invest "sweat" equity in creating their companies and then find it almost impossible to give up any ownership of them, chose to have the very largest piece of a tiny (and disappearing) pie rather than a smaller piece of what might have been a much larger pie.

Also along the food chain are a range of public–private, government-related programs, such as loan programs through the Small Business Administration, Small Business Innovation Research grants, and state-sponsored seed capital funds. The mindset among these groups is economic development focused on job creation and assistance to specific targeted groups of entrepreneurs or economically distressed areas. Entrepreneurs need to be ready not only to deal with a potential mountain of paperwork, but also be able to demonstrate the company's contribution to a locale's, region's, or state's economic well-being.

At the top of the food chain are venture capitalists, or VCs. To many entrepreneurs, VCs can appear to be "vulture" capitalists because they usually require a controlling interest in the companies in which they invest, a seat or two on the board, and/or some type of decision-making authority should the entrepreneur fail to hit financial milestones. But this view exists because entrepreneurs don't understand the role of the venture capitalist in the entrepreneurial process. VCs invest only in companies they believe can grow very large, very quickly. These firms usually pose much higher risks than others. The VCs mindset is strictly on return—no psychic income or economic development motivation or emotional commitment from them! Consequently, venture funds have extremely rigid investment guidelines, with extraordinarily liberal exception policies. They want companies capable of hitting the ball out of the park, firms with the potential to generate tremendous returns—at least ten times their money in five years. They need enormous returns from some of their bets because not all of their investments succeed. So in dealing with VCs, entrepreneurs need to show that their companies have great upside potential, and they may need to be willing to give up a significant chunk of equity for the money, experience, and contacts that VCs can bring to a fast-growth enterprise.

As entrepreneurs move up the food chain, they require ever-larger portions of capital to feed the growth of their companies. By understanding the mindset of different funding sources along the way, they will not only reduce their own frustration in the search for capital but, more important, increase their chances to secure the financing they need. And at some point, if they successfully cash out of their companies, they may become a source of financial food for others moving up the chain.

32

The Irritant
in the Oyster

The entrepreneur and the venture capitalist march to the beats of different drummers. The entrepreneur is always certain of success, and the venture capitalist is always cautious of the risks. Sometimes, as a result, the entrepreneur doesn't get the capital and the venture capitalist doesn't get the success, as Scott Cook found out when he tried to launch Intuit:

> *I figured this would be easy, to get venture capital funding. We knew the market well and we had done the research, and we had waited until we had the product partly done so we could show investors that there is not a technology risk here; it's actually up and running. But I was wrong on that one. In fact, nobody wanted to invest. We tried over 20 venture capital firms and we struck out with everyone.*

Striking out has happened at one time or another to everyone in the venture industry. Those venture firms that passed on Cook's software package, Quicken, missed out on a homerun product that produced a billion-dollar enterprise. Why is it that investors sometimes miss such spectacular successes? The nature of pearl making actually provides a perspective on this.

According to ancient lore, pearls were formed when moonlight-filled dewdrops fell into the ocean and were swallowed by oysters. What a wonderfully romantic notion!

Pearl making, however, is actually a messy, uncomfortable and time-consuming process. In the making of a pearl, an irritant, like a grain of sand, gets lodged in the shell of an oyster. The oyster reacts to this irritant by covering the foreign body with a crystalline substance called nacre to wall it off and keep it from irritating its soft insides. Over time, the oyster places concentric layers of nacre over the irritant until it forms a gem of unusual significance, quality, and value.

Venture investing is not unlike pearl making. An entrepreneur can be an irritant. The entrepreneur's unbridled optimism and stubbornness can blind him or her to risk. The entrepreneur's desire for control can make delegation impossible as an enterprise grows. The entrepreneur's insistence on doing things only his or her way can make him or her deaf to advice. The entrepreneur is often a foreign body in any structure that smacks of hierarchy and bureaucracy. And yet the entrepreneur is the driver in the processes of value and wealth creation because of his or her penchant for identifying and pursuing opportunity.

This is why venture capitalists continually look to invest in entrepreneurs. They count on entrepreneurs seeing things in the marketplace that they don't. Once they invest, they build around them types of concentric circles of talent, know-how, resources, and networks in the hopes of shaping an enterprise of unusual significance, quality, and value.

But the outcome is never certain. Not every oyster produces a pearl.

In a world where two big successes out of ten investments is considered excellent, the process of picking winners is more art than science. It continues to challenge, baffle, and mystify even the most experienced investors. Certain winners somehow fail; apparent losers sometimes win. Michael Moritz, a partner in the Sequoia Fund, captured the inherent unpredictability in venture capital this way: "While we may be surprised by a company's failure, we are consistently amazed by a company's great success."

Despite all the money, connections, industry knowledge, and experience that venture capitalists bring to an enterprise, venture investing remains a high-risk, high-reward business. Only a few companies have the management experience, product uniqueness, and market potential to attract the venture capitalists looking for the next pearl of entrepreneurial success. But those that do can be what business legends are made of.

33

Treading with Angels

D o you believe in angels? Entrepreneurs do. Not the Clarence, ring-a-bell, earn-your-wings kind of heavenly bodies. But the street-smart, been-there-done-that, got-rich kind of earthbound investors who seed startup companies.

Business angels are the answers to a lot of entrepreneurs' prayers for capital. Who are these mysterious beings? What types of petitions reach their ears? How do they affect entrepreneurs and the companies they choose to bless?

Many startup and emerging entrepreneurs find themselves in financial limbo. Not enough collateral to secure bank financing, yet not in need of large amounts of money to gain venture capital backing. After exhausting their own resources and perhaps some of the resources of family and friends, they still need capital to continue to grow. Thus, they look for angels.

These angels are wealthy individuals seeking promising investment opportunities. Many are former entrepreneurs who have successfully cashed out of their businesses. Others are professionals or corporate executives, now comfortably retired from their businesses, who have gained their wealth through their stock holdings and personal investments. Whatever their backgrounds before donning their haloes, they all bring two critical factors to the entrepreneurial process: financial wherewithal and a desire to get back in the game!

Finding and Petitioning Angels

As a result, business angels, preferring to stay close to home when they invest, have become the most important source of new venture funding in the United States. Estimates of angel investment in new and emerging ventures range as high as $50 billion annually, more than twice as much as venture capital investment. So there are lots of angels around. The challenge for the entrepreneur is twofold. The first is finding them. They aren't listed in the yellow pages and don't show up on the Web. The second is petitioning them. They have unique investment motivations and expectations that make them different from other sources of capital.

Andy Sack, who successfully raised $335,000 from angels for his company, Abuzz, in 1997, recommends a rule of thumb—only approach people who are less than two degrees of separation from you. "It's fine to approach people you know and get referred to another person," he advises. "However referrals of referrals rarely end up investing." Many entrepreneurs seek personal introductions to angels through professionals, like attorneys, who may have wealthy clients, and accountants, who may be aware of individuals who have recently cashed out of their businesses. Others seeking capital may be aware of successful entrepreneurs in their communities and seek a meeting with them, or attend venture fairs that attract both angels and venture capitalists, or go through associations of entrepreneurs for suggestions of individuals, or try to make contact with a member of an angel group, like the Band of Angels in Silicon Valley, or approach people whom they don't know but who they think may have a unique understanding of their businesses. An emerging source for identifying angel investors is online matching services that seek to match entrepreneurs with private and even institutional investors. Innovative private ventures, like Garage.com and Capitalyst.com, as well as publicly supported efforts, like AceNet, seek to provide access to capital for emerging companies. Their services have various levels of screening of ventures from none to several.

Petitioning business angels requires an understanding of their motivations for investing and their expectations of returns. Every angel invests to make money. However, angels will usually seek a smaller return and be more comfortable with a longer time frame than venture capitalists, somewhere in the range of 20 to 50 percent over five to ten years. Just as beneficial to the entrepreneur is the angel's preference usually not to seek a controlling interest in the company, thus leaving the entrepreneur in control of his or her enterprise.

Psychic Income

An angel has a different mindset from a venture capitalist about investing. Research has shown that angels invest for "psychic income." That is, they want to share in the excitement of launching a business, or they believe that they are giving back to their communities, or they want to help women and minority entrepreneurs, or they think the venture is socially or environmentally responsible, or for other nonmonetary reasons. I once introduced two women entrepreneurs to a business angel who visited their child-care business, which taught computer skills to preschoolers. The angel loved the business. Not only did he believe that it could make money, but he was thrilled with the idea of teaching very young kids computer skills and helping women entrepreneurs. So in pitching a deal to a prospective angel investor, an entrepreneur needs to communicate factors that might provide both psychic and financial return.

Andy Sack makes a key point about that first interaction with an angel. Although the angel will want to see a detailed business plan, he advises an initial personal meeting with the angel. "You want the investor's first impression of the business to be you and not a business plan," he says. "Angels invest in people and not in business plans." At that meeting, the entrepreneur's 10- to 20-minute presentation on the company is critical. It should focus on building excitement for and explaining the contributions of the venture, emphasize marketing strategy and tactics rather than stress the technological capabilities of the product or service, and present sound financial plans for the investor's capital.

Should the angel answer the entrepreneur's prayer for capital, then the relationship is not over; it's just beginning. Angels flock. As the company grows and requires more capital, the angel becomes a valuable contact to other angel investors, who may put in from $10,000 to $50,000 or more, individually or collectively, in an enterprise at any one time. Consequently, a savvy entrepreneur will involve the angel in the success of the enterprise by providing quarterly updates, discussing company achievements, and even sharing bad news, so the angel is not only not surprised but also can help with solving problems and taking advantage of opportunities.

In the best situations, angels don't just provide capital. They become a resource for the business, bringing their own experience and contacts to the venture, teaching the entrepreneur how to run a growing enterprise, and serving as a sounding board for the entrepreneur's ideas.

Companies fail sometimes because, to paraphrase an adage, entrepreneurs rush in where angels fear to tread. A well-networked, street-smart, and committed business angel on the shoulder of an entrepreneur can serve as a heavenly guardian for the entrepreneur in treading more wisely and carefully through the perils and possibilities of entrepreneurial growth.

34

Comedy, Tragedy, History

Entrepreneurship is an intensely human process. The endeavor of starting and building a company can tap a person's innermost desires and test a person's character. It can reveal strength and weakness, provide inspiration, or serve as a warning to others. Consequently, the stories of entrepreneurs not only can reveal insight into the company-building process but also can tell us something important about ourselves.

The noted sports journalist Tom Boswell said that he views all stories as Shakespeare viewed plays—as comedies, tragedies, or histories. Comedies focus on the amusing and enjoyable, and have a happy ending. Tragedies deal with struggle and defeat, and end in disaster. Histories recount the interplay of people, events, and issues over time.

Like Shakespeare's plays, the stories of entrepreneurs are in fact theatrical, like comedies, tragedies, or histories. At one end of attempts to create and develop a company lie elements of the comic: happiness, achievement, and a feeling of success. At the other end lie elements of the tragic: disappointment, failure, and a fall from grace for the protagonist.

Business as Comedy

Comedies, like *A Midsummer's Night Dream* and *Twelfth Night*, contain the unexpected, the surprising, and the unplanned for as plots turn and twist their ways to the inevitable resolution of issues and the happily-ever-after conclusion. Some of that same occurs in successful companies.

- Michael Dell starts out in his apartment selling computer peripherals as he's told by venture capitalists and others that he can't succeed. And yet, he becomes the classic entrepreneurial success story.
- Jack Stack turns a disastrous situation at Springfield ReManufacturing Corporation into one of the best companies to work for in America through determination, the financial education of all employees, and treating business like a game.
- Pleasant Rowland turns a love of dolls and history into a thriving enterprise at the company bearing her name.

Each of these examples, as well as others like them, emphasizes the possibilities of things, the ascendancy of the underdog, and the happy culmination of vision and work. As a result, these stories inform while they inspire.

Business as a Tragedy

Just as compelling, but for different reasons, is failure. Tragedies, like *Macbeth* and *Hamlet*, contain conflict, disaster, and misfortune. Companies that collapse, especially in spite of the best efforts of the founder, reveal the dark side of the entrepreneurial process.

- After two years of effort and the investment of their life's savings, a husband-and-wife team whom I know called it quits, remarking that shutting down the company was like losing a child. Their grief was as real as anything you'd see at a funeral.
- Bill Passman's company, Atherton Technologies, a software engineering firm in Silicon Valley, failed after consuming five years of his life and losing more than $10 million. The process made him an unhappy person without "a single friend left in the company."

Examples like these illustrate the loneliness, defeat, and dejection that can be part of an entrepreneurial endeavor. These are cautionary tales that can teach us what problems to look out for in our companies as well as how to be more aware of and deal with shortcomings in ourselves.

Business as History

Histories, like *Richard III* and *Henry IV*, reveal the impact of people, the effect of events, and the influence of issues in the shaping of organizations and institutions. By providing perspective and analysis, histories of companies and the people who shaped them can be extremely instructive in understanding why things happened the way the did.

Jim Collins and Jerry Porras provide a telling perspective on how great companies became great and sustained that greatness over time in their important book, *Built to Last*. Michael Lewis shows the dramatic influence that one person can have on events as he recounts in his book, *The New, New Thing*, how Jim Clark built Silicon Graphics, then Netscape, and then Healtheon into billion-dollar companies.

One of Shakespeare's famous lines observes, "All the world's a stage." In a real sense, all the company's a stage as well. The result is that the stories of entrepreneurs can engage us, just as good plays do, because they can inform, inspire, or challenge us while entertaining us.

As you think about your story, what would it be? Comedy, tragedy, or history? The way you view it will tell you something important not only about your company but also about yourself.

35

Wild and Crazy Guys

Some entrepreneurs remind me of "Two Wild and Crazy Guys," a skit that Steve Martin and Dan Aykroyd reprise occasionally on *Saturday Night Live*. The silly, funny, unconventional things they do and say make them unique and irrepressible. We may laugh at them and with them; we may shake our heads at their antics; we may be surprised by some of their comments. But we also recognize that they live in their own world with their own outlook on life. Entrepreneurs do something like this to create the culture of their organizations.

Entrepreneurs may seem crazy to people on the outside looking in to their companies. But if they're crazy, then they're crazy like foxes. Out of their surprising antics and counterintuitive actions come unique and strong cultures that serve to inspire and motivate employees and customers.

Wild and Crazy Things

Entrepreneurs who are not afraid to do apparently wild and crazy things not only create powerful cultures but also leave their own inimitable mark on their organizations. Some examples:

▎ *Traveling band.* Dennis Garberg has created a kind of "Nitty Gritty Dirt Band" with employees in his company, The Sunflower Group, a promotional services supplier. He plays lead (and only) harmonica. The band travels to the company's best customers and entertains them with music and barbecue to show their appreciation for their service. The employees say they get a real kick out of seeing their president and CEO rock-and-roll on the harmonica, even though Dennis knows he looks a little silly and says he is not really very good. So why does he do it? To encourage what he likes to call "reasonable risk-taking" in the company and to help create an environment that's both participatory and productive.

▎ *Glammy Awards.* Connie Suss and her partners run the Bijin Salon & Day Spa, a wellness and beauty center. In addition to events for employees like Hat Day, Wig Day, and Spring Madness Day, she orchestrates an annual "Glammy Awards." The evening celebrates the company's success by giving employees amusing prizes for everything from superior phone answering to giving great massages. In addition to recognizing the special attributes of employees, the awards reinforce the values that Connie and her partners believe are critical to success. Their goal with events like this is to create an environment in which employees can pursue "WOW!" reactions on a daily basis.

▌ *Golden Bell/Magic Bus.* Drew Hiss runs Paydata, a payroll processing service. He arranges fish fries and guided fishing trips for employees in the summertime. His other wild and crazy ideas include the "Golden Bell" that's rung in the office whenever an employee gets kudos from a customer or registers a new sales order. The bell rings a lot. He also surprises people with the "Magic Bus," a vehicle that magically appears now and then to take employees to a special lunch or even to a bowling alley, as a way to thank them for their efforts. Drew wants his employees to know that he values them.

▌ *Jeopardy game.* Tray Vedock, head of SKC Communication Products, a distributor of telecommunication equipment, loves to play a Jeopardy-type incentive game with employees to encourage a proactive attitude and increase sales. His prizes are unusual. The champion of one game won a month's car payment on his car. I'd like to get into that game! Tray wants his employees to know that a positive attitude and higher performance go together in his company.

▌ *Day trips.* Michael Carter is president of Carter Broadcasting Group, which manages radio stations. He surprises employees with day trips. One of the latest was to a local casino where employees were put in teams, given some cash, and told to work together to maximize their winnings. His philosophy is "together we win; together we lose." He wanted to reinforce the importance of that philosophy in his organization.

▌ *Fire walk.* Jeff Smith runs i2b Labs, a dot.com incubator. He gave employees in one of his companies the astonishing opportunity to walk over hot coals barefoot! He led the way, going first. Even those who were hesitant at first managed to get across. The event not only helped build relationships and enhance trust among his employees, but it also created a memorable life experience. People left believing that if they could walk barefoot across hot coals, they could do anything!

The Power of Culture

Entrepreneurs in successful companies create cultures that have meaning for employees. The meaning is a reflection of the entrepreneur's own values and beliefs. By daring to be a bit wild and crazy, by experimenting with events and activities, an entrepreneur learns what works and what doesn't in reinforcing the culture that he or she wants to create. At the same time, the wild and crazy things that entrepreneurs do to enhance culture form the mythology of a company. They become part of the story that communicates what's important around here and how people ought to act at work.

Entrepreneurs and employees in growth companies often tell me they want to be involved in an organization that's "fun." Entrepreneurs want to build a high-performing culture that they can enjoy, and employees want to work in a culture that's enjoyable to be part of. By being wild and crazy, entrepreneurs can achieve both.

36

PROFILE:
The Entrepreneur's Entrepreneur

Audrey MacLean is an entrepreneur's entrepreneur. She's done it all—startup, growth, venture backing, going public, investing—several times.

She co-founded her first company in 1982 in Silicon Valley when she was 30. After working for nine years in engineering, sales, and management positions for a networking company, she launched her own firm with a couple of colleagues to manufacture a line of switches for wide area networking products. After investing her own money and not taking a salary for over a year, she raised over $24 million through two rounds of venture capital and still managed to deliver her second child. When the company went public in 1987, however, she had less than 1 percent of it. First lesson learned: hold on to equity.

In her second high-tech firm, a manufacturer of high-speed switches, she retained over 20 percent of the common stock, cashed out with over $6 million, and decided to invest in other people's startups. After riding the rollercoaster of two growth companies nonstop for over 10 years, she opted to devote more time to her family. Second lesson learned: maintain balance.

Today, Audrey is the classic business angel. A nonjoiner, relishing her independence, she invests her own money in entrepreneurs in whom she comes to believe. Her record of success is impressive. She has picked winners in companies ranging from beer brewing to high technology to health care to education. Third lesson learned: back totally committed people.

Audrey's career as entrepreneur and angel was not always obvious. Raised in rural New York with nine younger brothers and sisters, her father saw a more traditional path for her. He refused to cosign a college loan for her to go to Columbia University because he believed that no one would marry her if she were in debt. After attending another college for a few years, she dropped out in her junior year, went to Paris, and modeled for fashion magazines for a while. Upon returning to the United States, she decided to head for California, where she completed college, earning a mathematics degree, and then went to work as an engineer and sales executive, before becoming an entrepreneur.

She has earned a reputation for toughness, directness, and honesty. Her philosophy of business building is straightforward: "Starting a company is like going to war. You can't do anything else but be fully engaged. You have to be insanely, passionately, nothing-can-stop-me committed"—as she was as an entrepreneur and as she expects those in whom she invests to be. Fourth lesson learned: be passionate.

She knows that with every investment she chooses to make her reputation is on the line. Consequently, like other effective angel investors, she takes an active coaching role in the firms in which she invests, backing people who genuinely want and seek help and advice. Financing about six startups annually, she will help write business plans, open doors to other companies to form strategic alliances, recruit experienced talent into the firms as they grow, find customers, and take a seat on the board. She will tap her extensive network to the VC community, other angels, and corporate partners to raise additional money for continued growth for the companies. Always, she will pose hard and challenging questions to entrepreneurs. As an affiliate in major venture capital funds, she will help them with due diligence on prospective investment opportunities, bring in deals (her own and others), and invest her own money in companies alongside that of venture capitalists.

In addition, Audrey stays involved in community initiatives, like improving schools in Silicon Valley, teaches an entrepreneurship course at Stanford University's Graduate School of Engineering (which is always oversubscribed), and serves on the board of the philanthropic Kauffman Center for Entrepreneurial Leadership, which is dedicated to accelerating entrepreneurship in America. Fifth lesson learned: give back.

To every endeavor in which she is involved, Audrey MacLean brings a brashness that springs from her own in-the-trenches success, an outspokenness that challenges assumptions and dispels pat answers, and a passion that is contagious for those with whom she interacts. Such are the attributes of an entrepreneur's entrepreneur.

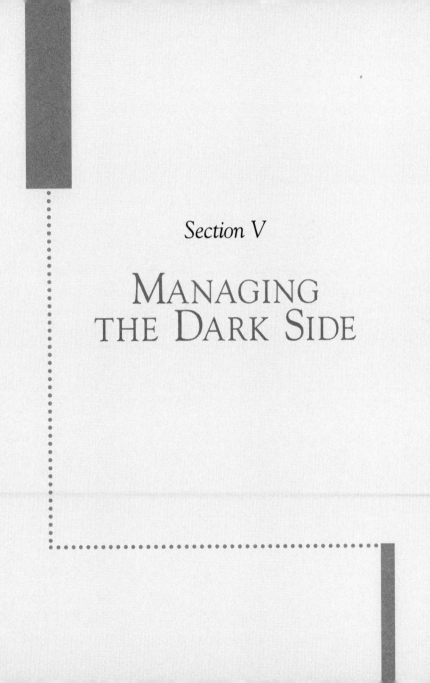

Section V

MANAGING THE DARK SIDE

37

Two Incontrovertible Facts

Two incontrovertible facts surround the entrepreneurial process. The first is this: companies fail!

Sometimes, they fail because entrepreneurs misread the market or underestimate their cash requirements or stop listening to customers or ignore good advice. Sometimes, in spite of great personal determination, adequate financial resources, and even obvious customer need, companies still don't make it because the timing for the product is wrong or a larger competitor steps in or the company grows too fast.

In any case, the failure of a company is a gut-wrenching experience for the entrepreneur. It was for me. I helped start a company in the security industry a few years ago. A CEO brought industry experience to the concept. I wrote the business plan and served on the board. A business angel wrote a check for $250,000. In 18 months, we pulled the plug on the company. The management team, which included family members of the CEO, knew how to train security guards and set up security systems, but not how to run a company. The firm began to burn cash as expenses outpaced revenues. Refusals to cut salaries drained resources further. Internal preferences for things like training equipment became more important than customer needs and wants. As the company spiraled downward, I had sleepless nights and confrontations with management. What had started with great expectations ended in disappointment and, ultimately, relief that it was over. The experience was painful. But it was also valuable. It taught me, as it teaches others in similar situations, a lot about what can go wrong in an entrepreneurial venture.

Failing Fast and Hard

A company is not just a structure for doing business. It is an extension of the ego of the entrepreneur and an expression of one's hopes and aspirations. It is an extremely personal endeavor that's tied to the entrepreneur's perception of himself or herself. This is why entrepreneurs tend to attribute success to their own efforts but, through a kind of internal self-protective mechanism, blame outside forces when their companies fail.

The husband-and-wife entrepreneurial team of Jeff and Millie Thomas put their hopes and aspirations into Kindertools, which makes safe products for infants and toddlers in Fort Collins, Colorado. Jeff called their startup venture "a scary kind of fun" since he quit his job as an accountant to devote all of his time to the enterprise. As the company struggled with the challenge of finding additional capital, Millie captured the personal nature of their venture and what it would feel like if it failed: "This product line is like our other child. If this doesn't make it, this will be a very grieving experience for us . . . it would be like losing a child."

No one knows for sure how many "children" of entrepreneurs are lost each year. Some estimates claim as many as four out of five companies fail during the first five years of business, whereas others are more positive, maintaining that six out of ten new businesses remain alive after seven years. The U.S. Department of Labor counted 863,699, 849,839, and 857,073 business terminations—that is, voluntary and involuntary closures—for the years 1995, 1996, and 1997, respectively. For those same years, the Administrative Office of the U.S. Courts identified 50,516, 53,207, and 53,826 business failures, respectively. Whatever the number, the message is clear; the opportunity to succeed carries with it the opportunity to fail.

If any entrepreneurs who were involved in these terminations, bankruptcies, and failures were blessed, it was those who failed fast and hard. Far better to go south rapidly than become one of the "walking wounded" or "living dead" who trudge on with no real prospects of success, sapping the time, energy, resources, and spirit of those involved with the venture.

Harsh but Good Teacher

Failure can be a harsh but good teacher, which leads to the second incontrovertible fact about the entrepreneurial process: failure is not an end. Many entrepreneurs who don't succeed the first time do indeed try again. They often bring to their second venture a wisdom, business savvy, and humility that may have been lacking in the first.

When Penny McConnell's cookie business declared bankruptcy in 1996, she recalled, "It hurt big time. I couldn't believe my little dream was gone." Faced with the problem of growing too fast, Penny's Pastries encountered production and cash flow difficulties. Rather than give up, she redefined what she wanted her company to be, focusing on smaller quantity, high-quality bakery goods, and restructured the enterprise to fit the style of life she wanted for herself and her employees. She now has a thriving venture in Austin, Texas.

Bill Passman's company, Atherton Technologies, a software engineering firm, failed after consuming five years of his life and losing more than $10 million of other people's money. After raising an easy $3 million in venture capital to launch the company, he experienced the heady feeling of a lot of entrepreneurs who go after the brass ring: "We felt like we were a member of the Silicon Valley elite, the gods-to-be, and ready to go on and conquer the world." But unwillingness to take advice and listen to customers ultimately brought Atherton down and made Passman an isolated and unhappy person without "a single friend left in this company." His response to Atherton's failure was to try again, only better. The result is that what he and others learned from the mistakes at Atherton provided the basis for wisdom as he launched and built Calico Technologies, now a very successful software design company in Silicon Valley.

Entrepreneurs who fail often reinvent themselves and come to view failure as a valuable learning experience.

If one has to fail, it's good to fail in the United States. At least, it's easier here. Unlike in other countries, failure is not a stigma here. U.S. laws are designed to encourage reorganization, and second efforts are admired. That attitude may be one of our most important and least appreciated competitive advantages. An entrepreneur can fail one week, and the next week walk into a bank for a loan to start again or talk to venture capitalists about funding yet another company.

In a real sense, the unwritten credo of entrepreneurs in Silicon Valley holds for entrepreneurs anywhere in the country. The only real failure is not to try!

38

Power Failure

As he sat across the table from me, he looked haggard and tired. He had been building his company for three years, but now it seemed like real work. "It's just not fun anymore," he told me. The excitement, energy, and enthusiasm with which he had launched his entrepreneurial venture were gone. Going to the plant in the morning was a chore; running the business was a drudgery; making decisions was a hassle. Everything seemed to irritate him. He had grown distant from his wife and family. This isn't what he expected when he started his company. What had gone wrong?

This entrepreneur, like some others who put in 80-hour weeks month after month and who apply every ounce of energy to making the company a success, had come to that proverbial wall that marathon runners encounter, that make-or-break point in the race when the mind and body just can't seem to go any farther. He was suffering an entrepreneurial power failure. He was burned out.

Telltale Symptoms

Burnout is not uncommon among entrepreneurs. Successful entrepreneurs bring an urgency, intensity, and work ethic to their ventures that are essential in starting and building viable enterprises. Ironically, these same strengths, unrelentingly pursued, can cause enormous stress that can eventually sap the will and spirit of the entrepreneur.

An interesting study by Richard Osborne in the early 1990s examined companies that had achieved profitable growth but had then failed to continue to grow. Although competitors and technological changes had stymied the growth of many companies in the study, surprisingly, the project discovered that in about one-third of the stalled companies the entrepreneurs "suffered a dissipation of their interest, energy, and aspiration" that prevented the companies from growing further. The study found that "18-hour days, exposure to risk, absentee parenthood, and a single-minded lifestyle that put business building ahead of all other responsibilities combined to undermine the owner-manager's commitment to the company he had created."

Entrepreneurial burnout has telltale symptoms. The entrepreneur may experience a loss of enthusiasm, a sense of being overwhelmed, feelings of anxiousness and fatigue, a loss of interest not only in the business but also in things outside the business. An all-out, don't-stop-for-a-breath focus on company building can wreak havoc on a marriage and family. In the best case, this approach results in missed family commitments, like tee-ball games and graduations, and perhaps an exhausted and resentful spouse. In the worst case, it can lead to separation or divorce. All of which puts additional stress on the entrepreneur.

Causes of Burnout

From my observation, two major and related factors cause entrepreneurs to burn out.

Entrepreneurs tend to be control addicts. In a sense, they have to be. They started their companies to be their own bosses, and at the start, they are usually in charge of everything, especially if they started on their own. But as a company grows, being in charge of everything becomes increasingly impossible to manage. So the entrepreneur faces the challenge of loosening his grip on the enterprise that is an extension of himself or herself. Letting go of parts of the company may be the greatest personal challenge the entrepreneur faces in managing his or her role as the leader of the organization.

At some point in the growth of an enterprise, an entrepreneur must ask himself or herself a key question: "What is it that only I can do?" Focusing on those critical—and few—activities or responsibilities can free the entrepreneur to do what he or she does best and usually most creatively. What I see successful entrepreneurs holding onto is the vision and values of the company as well as their particular personal gifts, like selling or product development or financing. Then they let go; they let others do the things at which they are not as good.

Related to control is decision making. Entrepreneurs tend to love to make decisions. I'm reminded of the story of the entrepreneur who boasted that she made a decision every 10 minutes in her company. When she was asked what happened if she made a wrong decision, she replied, "No problem. I just make another one."

At the start of a company, an entrepreneur makes all kinds of decisions, from which light bulbs to buy, to which phone system to use, to how to market, to which terms to make with investors. But as a company grows, the heady and exciting process of making every decision actually results in decision overload for the entrepreneur that eventually eliminates the advantage of speed in the marketplace that the company may initially have had.

There are ways to deal with burnout for the entrepreneur, but they take just as much preparation and commitment as when the entrepreneur launched the company. Entrepreneurs deal with their own power failures by resetting their business priorities, committing time to family, taking sabbaticals, and extending their networks. They renew their relationships with spouse and children, get involved with a new and different project in the company, take up golf or fly-fishing, bring their experience to a charitable activity, or take a leadership role in an entrepreneur support organization. In other words, they find something that can benefit from their participation and experience, and that can get their creative juices flowing again.

Entrepreneurs who recognize and deal with burnout are like those marathon runners who, when they hit the wall, find another reservoir of energy and enthusiasm that allows them to break through the wall, feel a renewed sense of challenge and purpose, and enjoy the race again.

39
Ruthless Perception

We had just completed a tour of his manufacturing plant and were talking about the growth of his company. He had started the firm out of his home and now had over 100 people and revenues of nearly $10 million in just three years. The company was continuing to expand at an increasing pace; the future was bright. As we talked about his ability to hold this tiger by the tail, he asked me, "Do you think I'm ruthless?"

I had come across this issue of ruthlessness before from entrepreneurs who were either in very rapid growth environments or in turnaround situations. I had a sense of what was behind his question.

Explosive Growth and Desperate Turnaround

I told him that I did not think he was ruthless, and asked him why he had asked the question. He said that his wife had told him she thought he was becoming "a little ruthless" in building the company. He had recently let go an employee who was with him at the start of the company back when he was struggling to develop his product and find customers. She could not understand why her husband had fired him.

He explained to me that the employee could not grow with the company despite the entrepreneur's best efforts to give him more responsibility, to coach him, and to provide training for him. The employee's skills were limited, and as the company grew, the entrepreneur had to bring in more talented, experienced managers who could take the company to the next level of growth. The result was that the company was passing the employee by, and he was becoming increasingly bitter. His bitterness was negatively affecting others in the company, and so he had to go.

Entrepreneurs in two types of situations run the risk of being perceived as ruthless—during heady and chaotic explosive growth, and during desperate turnaround efforts. In the first case, an entrepreneur may be required to bypass the very people who had helped start his or her enterprise to ensure continued growth of the firm. In the second case, an entrepreneur may be required to cut costs and trim payroll to ensure the survival of the company.

I've never met an entrepreneur who enjoyed bypassing people, especially those who were committed to his or her enterprise in its startup phase, or who took pleasure in letting people go to cut costs. Just the opposite in fact is true. Entrepreneurs tend to take pride in seeing those around them grow personally and succeed financially.

In building a company, two obligations dictate the actions and decisions of an entrepreneur and often determine whether he or she will be perceived as ruthless.

An Entrepreneur's Obligations

The first obligation is to do what is best for the company. To maintain high growth, an entrepreneur must recruit and retain talent. Often those who start with the company do not have the experience to manage it as it doubles in size, then doubles again, then doubles again. They have not previously developed the kinds of policies and procedures that are essential to ever-larger enterprises, or created multiple product offerings, or gone global in marketing efforts. Consequently, the entrepreneur must find and hire people who can bring the kind of experience and expertise to the company that can ensure its continued success.

In turnaround situations in which a company is on the brink of failure or faces a life-or-death crisis, the entrepreneur must often act autocratically in making unpopular decisions. The very survival of the firm is at stake. The first requirement is usually to stop bleeding financially, which means slashing payroll to cut costs to keep the company afloat. In this situation, it's always best to make the first cuts deep enough so that later cuts may not be necessary.

The second obligation is to take care of the people. In fast-growth companies, entrepreneurs may set up opportunities for leadership and management training for employees; provide mentoring and coaching; and, especially important, be up front about an employee's strengths, areas for development, and chances of promotion.

In the turnaround environment, an entrepreneur can provide placement assistance, severance packages, and counseling to assist those who are displaced.

In either case, despite an entrepreneur's best efforts to serve both the company and the employees, he or she still runs the risk of being perceived as ruthless. That comes with the territory of company leadership. What can help an entrepreneur deal with the charge, whether from an employee or a spouse, is an internal fortitude, a proactive approach in dealing with employees, and a belief that one is doing the right thing. Although those may help the entrepreneur continue to move forward, they won't make bypassing dedicated employees or letting good people go any less painful.

40

Kicked Up or Out

What happens when a company stops performing? What happens when projections are missed for two, three, and four consecutive quarters; when sales drop off precipitously; when uncollected accounts receivable mount; when orders stop coming in; when expenses continuously outstrip revenues? Often, heads roll. And if the entrepreneur does not have controlling interest in the enterprise, then his or her head is likely to roll first!

The head of a friend of mine in Austin, Texas, rolled not long ago. He had been an engineer with a Fortune 100 company and had invented a new diagnostic medical device. When the firm he was with decided not to do anything with the invention, it let him have the patent. He was convinced the device had potential, so he gave up the security of a regular paycheck to launch his own venture. As president, CEO, and chairman, he worked literally day and night developing the manufacturing, establishing a client base among physicians, creating alliances with teaching hospitals, and securing capital from private investors. Along the way, he had to give up controlling interest in the company to get the capital he needed to grow. After four years, he took his first vacation. When he returned from Jamaica, he learned the board had called a special meeting, replaced him as president, CEO, and chairman, and made him "Chief Scientist" by putting him in charge of designing new products. The board had decided that the firm under his leadership was not progressing satisfactorily, that the company had outgrown his abilities to manage it, and that a change needed to be made. So they brought in a professional manager with experience in growth companies, and shaped a new, and what they believed to be more appropriate, role for the entrepreneur.

Pressure to Perform

To say the least, he was shocked by this turn of events. But he should not have been completely surprised. The company was progressing much more slowly than he told investors it would. He was having a hard time delegating. He was slow to bring in new talent to the firm.

In situations like this, entrepreneurs, like my friend, risk being kicked up or out of their own companies. The dramatic and sometimes unexpected change in roles can be a gut-wrenching experience for the person who has invested his or her time, energy, and resources into starting and building a company.

In firms that are designed for very rapid growth and require large amounts of capital, such as venture-backed enterprises, the pressure to perform is extremely high. Financial projections are promises the entrepreneur makes to investors. If he or she keeps breaking those promises, then something has to give. Often it is the position of the entrepreneur. Boards of directors will replace, "kick out," founders who fail to perform as expected to get companies back on track. In making the best of a bad situation, good boards make their expectations explicit, are up front with the entrepreneur, and seek to minimize surprise. But it is not uncommon for a board to act on a spur of the moment to initiate a radical change in the structure and operation of a company.

In other cases, boards may seek to restructure the role of the entrepreneur in the company—to "kick up" the founder. So the entrepreneur may become "Chief Scientist" or chairman or vice chairman. In other words, the board seeks to retain the vision and energy of the entrepreneur in some capacity while removing the entrepreneur from any actual management responsibility in the operation of the company. This can be good for the entrepreneur as well as the company, if indeed, the company has outgrown the abilities of the entrepreneur to manage it. But the change usually does not come easily for the entrepreneur, who is faced with the reality of giving up on the idea of running his or her own company.

Dealing with the Shift in Control

Doug Kahn, a very talented entrepreneur who has grown several successful companies, understands the incredible momentum to move forward that comes with venture backing and the decision to go public. His advice to other entrepreneurs about the right time to go public is clear—when the entrepreneur is convinced that he or she can deliver sustained earnings for the next three to four quarters. This is because the market and Wall Street analysts will monitor the performance of the company and be cruel on it if it fails to live up to expectations. With outside investors, like venture capitalists and the public marketplace, the locus of control in a company changes dramatically. According to Kahn, if the entrepreneur misses projections in the first quarter, he or she can expect to be "questioned"; in the second quarter, expect to be "jumped on"; in the third quarter, expect to be "crucified"; and in the fourth quarter, expect to be "gone!" That's the reality of a shift in control of the company from the entrepreneur to other investors.

What can an entrepreneur do to avoid being kicked up or out? First, he or she can retain control of the company. By tapping their own funds, growing internally, and using the capital of family, friends, and private investors, who usually ask for less equity than venture capitalists, entrepreneurs may be able to get the money they need to grow without giving up control of the company to others.

If retaining control is not possible, then the entrepreneur must understand that a shift in control has taken place, that he or she will be expected to meet or exceed financial projections, and that the leadership of the company now includes managing a board as well as other aspects of the enterprise.

Every effective entrepreneur has a voice in selecting board members, maintains good lines of communication with them, finds ways to learn and grow as a manager of an expanding enterprise, and seeks and heeds good advice. In so doing, the entrepreneur can continue to maintain his or her role as the leader of the company.

41

Lonely at the Point

In the midst of constant activity, amid a swirl of interactions with employees, customers, and suppliers, an entrepreneur can experience the most unexpected feeling in running a company—a feeling of being completely and totally alone.

When the entrepreneur encounters a situation he or she may never have faced before, when exhaustion and worry begin to cloud decision making, when the company loses its best customer, when the bank calls the loan, or when any other critical personal or organizational issue confronts the company, the entrepreneur must ask himself or herself that memorable question from the *Ghostbusters* movie, "Who ya gonna call?" For the person who is trying to build a successful venture, it's not always an easy question to answer.

The Danger of Loneliness

The entrepreneur usually hesitates to talk to a spouse to avoid worrying him or her about the status of the company in which they are both invested. The entrepreneur avoids raising company-threatening issues with employees since he or she does not want to damage morale or lessen commitment to the enterprise. The entrepreneur won't discuss critical issues with investors because he or she does not want them to think their investment is in jeopardy. The entrepreneur may not feel comfortable talking to board members since he or she alone wants to solve the problem to demonstrate his or her competence in running the organization. So who's left to talk to? As one entrepreneur told me about what it is like to be constantly out front of the company, "It really is lonely at the point."

Loneliness carries with it a danger. Unless the entrepreneur finds someone in whom he or she can confide, someone who can be trusted with innermost concerns, someone who can really listen and then provide useful feedback, then the entrepreneur runs the risk of becoming isolated. The danger in being cut off from those who may be able to provide perspective on concerns and solutions to issues is the development of a fortress mentality that reinforces the feeling of loneliness. An entrepreneur who had launched a fast-growth software venture told me what it was like for her at times in dealing with the endless challenges that are part of company building: "Sometimes I think of that line from the Elvis song, 'I'm so lonely I could cry.'"

Dealing with Loneliness

Smart entrepreneurs find ways to deal with loneliness. Some may establish relationships with mentors. If an entrepreneur can find a mentor with been-there, done-that experience, one who can listen without trying to tell his or her own war stories, and a person who has a genuine desire to see the entrepreneur succeed, then the entrepreneur can tap a font of street-savvy wisdom that can boost his or her own morale while providing practical solutions to key issues that the company may be facing and networks to others who may be able to contribute to the company's development. Many seasoned entrepreneurs, if asked, are more than willing to provide counsel and advice to emerging entrepreneurs, as long as the upstarts don't take advantage of their time or contacts.

Other entrepreneurs set up ad-hoc advisory boards of professionals who may or may not actually meet as a group. These advisors may come from various disciplines like accounting, law, finance, public relations, marketing, direct mail, human resources, and international business. Many professionals set aside pro-bono time to work with emerging entrepreneurs in the hope that once they are successfully established they will become paying clients. Entrepreneurs call on these professionals for recommendations on specific issues related to their unique knowledge and expertise.

One of the most personally meaningful ways that entrepreneurs deal with loneliness is by joining an association of entrepreneurs like the Young Entrepreneurs' Organization, the Council of Growing Companies, or the Young Presidents' Organization. Though each has different requirements for membership, they all share one powerful mechanism for shared learning and support—

small, organized groups of entrepreneurs who meet on a regular basis to share personal and organizational issues in a confidential and trusting atmosphere. Most participants in these forums and chapters indicate that this experience is the most important resource for them in building their companies and renewing their spirits. As members of a forum or chapter come to know each of the other entrepreneurs and their companies, they share experiences, tell lessons learned, provide motivation, and deliver candid, and sometimes harsh, feedback to each other in dealing with issues facing their companies. The real message of the forum or chapter is that the entrepreneur is not alone!

Company building is a marathon, not a race. To avoid the loneliness of the long-distance runner, an entrepreneur needs to tap the support and experience of others. The entrepreneurial course is not only easier to traverse but also more enjoyable to run with others cheering one along.

42

Love and Fear

Entrepreneurs are a driven lot. They exhibit a persistent, restless, almost obsessive striving to succeed. They demonstrate a compulsiveness to make their ventures survive and thrive, and an obstinance to endure in the face of the unexpected.

This determination not to give up, to create something of significance, to build a viable enterprise springs from the two great motivators of entrepreneurial achievement: love and fear. Love and fear are the two sides of entrepreneurial drive—sometimes spurring fanatical devotion to a worthy cause and at other times sparking near terror from being associated with a lost cause.

Doing What You Love

Most entrepreneurs start their ventures by doing something they love. Jeff Bezos was fascinated with books and then launched Amazon.com. Jim Stowers's interest in financial instruments led him to build American Century into a $100 billion mutual fund company. Pleasant Rowland was always enamored of both history and doll making, so she created a company to make dolls with period costumes and histories to match. Richard and James Cabela's enjoyment of the great outdoors led the brothers to turn a hobby of hand-tying fishing flies into a leading sports equipment catalog and retail operation.

To do what one loves, one must first identify what that is:

▌ *Don't take for granted what you are good at.* Debbi Fields made cookies as a child, became an exceptional baker, and then started Mrs. Fields Cookies. Danny O'Neill thinks of coffee as wine connoisseurs think of wine, actually picked coffee beans, and then started a gourmet coffee business, The Roasterie.

▌ *Use your experience.* Try something on a smaller scale or on someone else's payroll to determine where your passion lies. Jim McCann owned a few flower shops in New York to understand the business and his role in it before he launched 1-800-FLOWERS. Others may work for a larger company in an industry before starting their own companies in the same industry.

▌ *Get feedback.* Find out from others where they think your real talents lie. Friends kept telling Rich Davis that the barbecue sauce he would make on weekends was really terrific. He eventually gave up his job as a college professor to make the sauce on a full-time basis and to build KC Masterpiece.

Successful entrepreneurs have the ability to create meaning for others through what they love to do. Mrs. Fields Cookies is not in the cookie business! It's in the "feel-good" business; the feel-good happens to come in the form of a cookie. Maggie Moos ice cream shops don't sell just ice cream; they sell an experience as one peers through the glass to watch the crush-ins being mixed with a favorite flavor. And American Century is not in the business of selling mutual funds; it's in the business of helping people become financially independent.

Because entrepreneurs do what they love, they don't have any trouble getting up in the morning and going to work! Just as important, doing what one loves helps an individual stay focused and even calm amid the certain ups and downs, the inherent unpredictability, and inevitable setbacks that are part of the entrepreneurial process.

Fear of Failure

Just as powerful as love in motivating entrepreneurs is fear.

Possible bankruptcy, loss of one's major customer, the inability to make a key product work, violating financial covenants, and losing key personnel can give entrepreneurs an eyes-in-the-headlights look as they realize that their ventures may belly-up. For entrepreneurs, organizational failure is personal failure. The prospect of failure can be terrifying to people who want to build companies and for individuals whose companies are extensions of their own egos.

Ironically, for many entrepreneurs in these situations, nothing may succeed like the fear of failure.

Max Carey has built CRD in Atlanta into one of the largest sales training companies in the country. But he was able to do this only because he nearly failed, as he points out in his book, *The Superman Complex*. At the start, CRD was an undercapitalized, generic sales training company pitted against much larger and more well-known competitors. Unable to get profitable contracts with major firms, the company was failing, so much so that Max personally went into debt and the bank repossessed his car.

Looking back today, Max says, "I thank God for my early failures." For him, as for other entrepreneurs, impending failure was a terrific motivator. Personally, it made him more willing to experiment—desperation can do that. Organizationally, it caused the firm to abandon a way of business that was not working—a sense of reality can do that. The result was that CRD began to use customers of major firms to determine how the salespeople in those firms should be trained and how products should be presented. This approach revolutionized sales training and provided CRD with a reputation as a sales training company that produced amazing results.

When You Are on the Brink

Max Carey's experience provides insight for others who may be on the brink of collapse:

▌ *Take off the rose-colored glasses.* Face up to the fact that something is fundamentally wrong.

▌ *Recognize the red flags that are waving.* Pretending that a problem does not exist or hoping that it will simply go away—whether it's a quality defect, an employee who is the proverbial rotten apple in the barrel, or poor cash flow—leads to disaster.

▌ *Seek candid criticism of what's going wrong.* Talk to your employees, customers, and vendors.

▌ *Involve others in finding a solution.* Multiple heads are indeed better than one.

▌ *Experiment.* Test alternate approaches and strategies.

For entrepreneurs building viable enterprises, love is very good, but fear is also often necessary. The former provides the warmth that emanates from the fire of commitment; the latter provides the chill that comes facing cold reality.

43

PROFILE:
Talent for a Time

She started her company in Silicon Valley in 1990. She had a technology background with degrees in mathematics and computer science, brought some sales and marketing experience from a stint with another software company, and wrote a credible business plan for a software applications company. She jumped into the business-building process enthusiastically; financing the startup with her own money and some capital from friends; working at a fevered pitch to develop the product, expand the management team, and solidify business partnerships.

Over the next three years, the company grew and began to attract the attention of venture capital firms in the area. To fuel the continued growth of the company and to get it to the stage where she could take it public, she began to realize she would need a significant infusion of additional capital. So she started talking to venture capitalists looking for opportunities in the software industry. After nearly a year of negotiation, she struck a deal with a major venture firm that brought not only its capital but also capital from several larger corporations that wanted to establish strategic alliances with her company to gain access to her technology. It was an excellent deal for everyone. She got the capital she needed, and the investors had a stake in a promising growth enterprise. But with the deal came a change in the locus of control of the company. She no longer had controlling interest. A board of directors now represented the investors who had the controlling interest of the company.

She lasted a little over a year as president and CEO. Then the board changed her role, making her chairman of the board, effectively kicking her up in the organization to remove her from any management or operational responsibilities. What had happened?

I will not use her real name, instead calling her Helen, because the story of her "ouster," as she calls it, is still very personal for her. But it is a story that is revealing of what can happen when control of a company shifts from the entrepreneur to other investors.

Steve Lazarus, an outstanding venture capitalist who heads up Arch Venture Partners and a member of several boards of growth companies, has identified three duties of an effective board member. He maintains a board member must have (1) a duty of care, that is, to do the work that is required to fully understand the issues of the company; (2) a duty of loyalty, that is, to act in a way that serves the best interests of all the shareholders; and (3) a fiduciary responsibility to ensure the legal and ethical operation of the firm. In this context, the great moment in the life of a board—

when it has the fate of a company most directly in its hands—is when it decides to hire or fire the CEO. This involves making an assessment of whether the CEO can move the company to the next level of growth and success.

In Helen's case, the board decided that she could not. What made this decision so painful for her at the time was the fact that just six weeks before their decision at the regularly scheduled board meeting, the board seemed to give her a vote of confidence in encouraging her to move forward with an important contract negotiation. She was in the midst of discussions with a large corporation for distribution of the company's software, and as she learned later, the board did not want to do anything that might jeopardize that negotiation. So instead of communicating their concerns about the slower-than-anticipated growth of the company and their doubts about her management abilities, they opted to wait to see what would happen to these sensitive negotiations with the larger firm.

As it turned out, the negotiations went well and the contract was signed. The board then took what to her was the greatest surprise of her entrepreneurial career—the decision to remove her from a direct management role in the company and replace her with someone who brought more extensive experience in managing rapid growth companies.

As she looks back, she realizes now that there were some telltale signs that the board was losing confidence in her management skills. Board members would meet for "preboard" meetings without her to discuss issues of the company. New board members would be brought on without consultation with her. There were increasing questions about why the company was not hitting its projections. But she was so busy building the company, so tied up in the day-to-day issues of trying to run the enterprise, that, she says now, she never noticed her increasing distance from the board. "I did not survive as CEO," she says, "because I lost touch with my board."

Today, Helen is not bitter because she made a critical decision during her transition in the company. She decided not to fight the change. She decided this for two reasons. First, it was never her intention to remain president and CEO forever. She just expected it to last longer than it did, and thus she thought that this might be best for the company.

Steve Lazarus has observed in his experience that some entrepreneurs have "a talent for a time." That is, he or she fits the role of CEO for a while, but then the company outgrows that talent and someone else is needed to take the company to its next stage of development. He argues that it is essential for the entrepreneur and especially the lead director of the board to have fair and open discussions about this to determine the role for the entrepreneur that best serves the company.

Her second reason for going along with the change was her fear that a huge battle would destroy what she had worked so hard to build and would hurt others in the company to whom she felt committed. She saw herself as "an exceptional builder." In her role as chairman of the board, she could still have an important role in the company, continue to influence the culture and values she had helped to create, and perhaps, from a very different perspective, learn more about the enterprise process.

Today, Helen indicates that she has a good relationship with both the CEO who replaced her and the board. She has used this experience to become a more savvy and insightful businessperson. And what has she learned? An entrepreneur should conduct his or her own due diligence on every board member to learn the strengths and weaknesses of each, be assertive in building a personal relationship with each board member to understand his or her individual concerns, emphasize the importance of open communication on issues critical to the company's development, and appreciate how hard it is for an entrepreneur to disconnect from the enterprise that he or she started.

As a director now, not only of her company but also of others, Helen believes that her experience with her own transition will serve her well in helping other entrepreneurs grow into ever-wider management responsibilities or be more prepared than she was for a transition, when their talent for a time comes to an end.

Section VI

SOCIAL IMPACT OF ENTREPRENEURSHIP

44

Of Pies and Wealth

The numbers are amazing. The United States boasts about 270 billionaires, 250,000 deca-millionaires, and 5 million millionaires. We are in the greatest period of wealth creation in our history. Who's creating all this wealth? For the most part, entrepreneurs.

A 1997 study on "The Rich and the Poor: Demographics of the U.S. Wealth Distribution" by John Weicher for the Federal Reserve Bank of St. Louis Review found that "most of the nation's rich are entrepreneurs in the American tradition." It concluded: "Concern over the concentration of wealth should be tempered by the apparent fact that 'the rich' are a changing group, even over rather short periods, and by the fact that they are . . . entrepreneurs."

Michael Stolper in his book, *Wealth: An Owner's Manual*, reinforces this finding. He points out only three ways to become wealthy—win the lottery, save money over a long period, or own your own business. More and more people today are finding that owning one's own business is not only a way to fulfill one's passion but also the way to wealth.

The New Wealthy

Much of this wealth is very new and in the hands of rather young people. The six college friends who started Excite on the Internet in 1993 sold it in 1999 for $7 billion. Jeanette Symons who co-founded Ascend Communications in 1989 sold it in 1999 for $20 billion. Ashu Roy and Gunjan Sinha sold their online directory WhoWhere in 1999 and collected $40 million each. Jerry Yang and David Filo, the co-founders of Yahoo, are each worth about $3 billion. Jeff Bezos of Amazon.com is worth over $5 billion. All these entrepreneurs and others are reshaping the way wealth is created and even distributed.

The traditional analogy of the wealth creation process referred to the image of an expanding pie. It emphasized that wealth is not static, that what accrues to one person does not have to be taken from someone else. Wealth is dynamic and continues to grow—like an ever-larger pie.

A better analogy today is the creation and expansion of many pies simultaneously. Some pies are larger than others, but all contribute to the wealth of the nation as a whole. The bakers are the entrepreneurs who are innovating, who are pushing the edges of technology, who are pursuing opportunity.

Culture of Ownership

Equally important, entrepreneurs are sharing their pies with those who are providing the ingredients. Employee ownership is becoming commonplace in fast-growth companies where entrepreneurs are turning employee stock ownership into a basic building block for startup enterprises.

Dr. J. Robert (Bob) Beyster, the Johnny Appleseed of employee stock ownership, started his company, Scientific Applications International Corporation (SAIC), in San Diego in 1969 as a scientific consulting firm with a dozen employees. From the beginning, Beyster insisted on sharing equity: "I wanted to build a company where people would be incentivized to stay, and when the going got tough, they wouldn't run out the door." Today, SAIC has over 40,000 employees and $5 billion in annual revenues. Beyster has 1.5 percent of the company. "We turn employees into stakeholders," he says. "It makes a difference, and it's the right thing to do."

Does it make a difference? In a survey of Entrepreneur Of The Year winners conducted by the Kauffman Center for Entrepreneurial Leadership, 42 percent of the firms responded that they provided stock ownership to employees, whereas 58 percent did not. In terms of financial performance, firms that provided for employee stock ownership did better. Firms providing their employees with ownership positions had higher sales growth (57 percent faster growth) and higher gross profit margins (38 percent higher margins).

What Bob Beyster, the entrepreneurs in Silicon Valley, and the 10,000 companies with employee stock ownership plans are responding to is an expanding culture of ownership in the American workforce. Today's employees are increasingly prepared to bet on their own performance, increasingly willing to accept the risks and rewards of the entrepreneurial process, and increasingly expecting to have a share of the pies they help produce.

I have a cousin in Denver who represents this culture. A software engineer with a family and two small children, he recently left a firm because the entrepreneur who founded the company provided no stock ownership opportunities for his employees. So my cousin opted to go with another emerging company at a lower salary because it provided stock options for him. He chose to take a longer-term view, give up the security of his current employment, and take a chance on a promising growth company that made him a stakeholder in its success. There are lots more like him.

Golden Age of Philanthropy

And what will those who accumulate wealth do with it? Will they focus on conspicuous consumption and simply be perceived as the new robber barons or will they use their wealth for the benefit of society? I suspect the latter.

Bob Beyster used his wealth to start his Foundation for Enterprise Development to encourage others to share equity. Ewing Kauffman invested his resources in the Ewing Marion Kauffman Foundation to promote youth development and accelerate entrepreneurship in America. Jerry Yang and David Filo have become the youngest contributors to fund a chair in entrepreneurship at the Stanford Engineering School. Dick Schulze established the Schulze Family Fund and the Best Buy Children's Foundation. Pierre Omidyar set up the eBay Foundation with 107,000 shares of presplit eBay stock. Many others are using their wealth to shape a new and creative social entrepreneurship focused on performance, outcomes, and experimentation. They are beginning to bring their own entrepreneurial know-how and experience to a variety of specific social problems, and insisting on becoming personally involved in the initiatives they choose to fund.

Many of today's wealthy entrepreneurs are young and still running their companies. As they mature and as they take the time to give back to the society that has enabled their success, they have the opportunity to bring a new, entrepreneurial leadership to the social sector. The great wealth that entrepreneurs have generated at the close of the twentieth century could lead to a golden age of philanthropy in the twenty-first.

45

Identity,
Belonging, Security

E ntrepreneurship is more than an economic phenomenon. It is a force that creates social value and a resource for community development.

In "Building Community," Medal of Freedom winner John Gardner presents an insightful examination of the importance of community and a provocative analysis of the need individuals have for identification with and empowerment within the communities in which they live. He emphasizes that "Where community exists it confers upon its members identity, a sense of belonging, a measure of security." I am convinced that entrepreneurship can help confer identity, belonging, and security not only on those who elect to start and grow enterprises but also on those who join them in that effort and on the wider environment in which they operate.

Community Builders

Consider Rick Krska. He was caught up in the nationwide downsizing movement of major corporations. He and a number of his colleagues came to believe that they were corporate misfits. So they built a company from his basement that shaped a new community for themselves.

Observe Roberto Alfaro. He lives among the gangs in the Mission District of San Francisco where, he says, "Everybody in here has friends that have died, someone who's been hurt in some way or another." He started a business to create a stronger sense of belonging among gang members.

Reflect on Jack Stack. He and 119 other employees were in desperate straits of losing their jobs when International Harvester decided to eliminate the division where they worked. So they pooled their resources and bought the company with a staggering 89:1 debt-to-equity ratio to provide security for themselves and their families.

Each of these people is quite different from the others. But they have two important characteristics in common. Each is an entrepreneur. And each is a community builder.

Egalitarian Avenue to Self-Sufficiency

Today, in many parts of our country, we face a breakdown of community. Too many of our inner cities seem torn from within and abandoned from without. Displaced workers rightfully worry about their futures while too many of our youth waver between apathy and anger. The problems that plague our society are profound and

complex. There are no simple solutions. Entrepreneurship is certainly not a panacea. But I am convinced that it is one effective
and proven way to confer "identity, a sense of belonging, a measure of security." In other words, it can contribute to the hopeful
and renewing process of building community. Entrepreneurship
contributes to this process because it is a genuinely egalitarian
avenue to self-sufficiency and independence. One does not need
to be degreed, certified, or accredited to be an entrepreneur.

Rick Krska and his corporate misfits, determined to create a
viable enterprise, have grown their company, LaserCycle in
Lenexa, Kansas, a remanufacturer of toner and ink jet cartridges,
into one of the leading firms in their industry. The company now
provides identity for over 120 employees and their families.

Roberto Alfaro says his T-shirt business, Latinismo, is "about
peace among gang members here in the city." A youth activist in
the District maintains that "entrepreneurship is one of the best
alternatives for communities such as the community in the Mission . . . where they're cut off from mainstream business, where
they don't have the networks or the history or the connections."

Jack Stack and the other employee-owners of Springfield
ReManufacturing Corporation, now recognized as one of the best
companies to work for in America, have created a successful high-
growth company that has not only provided security for them, but
also become a major community resource for Springfield, Missouri.

Because of the power of entrepreneurship not only to create
jobs but also to build community, we see today a proliferation of
community-based organizations designed to assist and facilitate
the startup process, the commitment of an increasing number of

foundations to fund and support initiatives in entrepreneurship, and an expansion of training and education programs in entrepreneurship based on the notion that it is better to teach someone how to fish than to give him or her fish.

Ethic of Community

I've heard it suggested that individuals in black market activities and illegal trades, like drug dealers, are gifted entrepreneurs because of their willingness to take risk, their adeptness at serving "customers," and their skill at certain business functions, such as distribution. They are not. Those who prey on the addictions, weaknesses, or fears of others are destroyers of community. They cause others to lose their identities, to feel alone and ostracized, and to act out of apprehension and insecurity. True entrepreneurs are builders of community whose ethical base includes a desire to help create self-sufficient people in healthy communities.

Entrepreneurship is a force for community health and well being. It does confer "identity, a sense of belonging, a measure of security." Rick Krska now knows where he and his associates fit. Roberto Alfaro is rebuilding his community and helping others feel part of that renewal. Jack Stack and those with whom he works have found out that they can be safe in their own performance.

I admire each of them—as entrepreneurs and as community-builders. Each of them, like so many other entrepreneurs, has not only helped produce self-sufficient people but also enhanced the quality of life in the communities in which they operate.

46

Valuable Possession

Over the past decade, a new and more positive image of the entrepreneur has emerged. The person who starts and builds an enterprise, pursues opportunity, handles adversity, and creates value has become an individual who is deserving of honor.

To me, "honor" is the outcome of significant accomplishment and credible conduct. It is the coming together not only of what we do but also of how we do it. Accomplishment marks one's ability to do something well, to perform. Conduct speaks to one's character.

In the film, *In Search of Bobby Fisher*, a young chess prodigy learns to play chess brilliantly. In the process, however, he must come to terms with how he will play the game—with his character, with his view of himself as a player. In the most powerful scene in the movie, he performs an act that makes him deserving of honor. He sees the outcome of his championship match and knows that he will win. But because of the way he chooses to play the game, he offers through a handshake across the chessboard—a surprising and unconventional gesture in match play—to share victory with this opponent. For him, he combined significant accomplishment with credible conduct.

Values and Morals in Entrepreneurship

The stereotypical image that can sometimes hover around the concept of the entrepreneur is one of a conniving, step-on-anyone-to-get-ahead, wheeler-dealer—a kind of J. R. Ewing personality—who cares for no one but himself and nothing but his own advancement. No doubt there are some individuals like that in the business world. And we do hear the term *entrepreneur* occasionally applied to scam artists who rip off unsuspecting people, to dealers in illegal trades who prey on the weaknesses of others, and to white-collar criminals who try to cheat the system. But applying the term *entrepreneur* to people in these types of transactions implies that the term has no basis in values and morals. This is a wrong way to think about the concepts of entrepreneur and entrepreneurship.

Entrepreneurship is not a values-free, amoral process. If we recognize the entrepreneur as the leader of an organization, then Ronald Heifetz, the director of the Leadership Education Project at the John F. Kennedy School of Government at Harvard University, provides an important insight into the moral basis of the entrepreneur. In his important book, *Leadership Without Easy Answers*, he points out that "There is no neutral ground from which to construct notions and theories of leadership because leadership terms, loaded with emotional content, carry with them implicit norms and values." He maintains that leadership is more than influence, prominence, and authority. Leadership is an activity in which the leader mobilizes people to do something socially useful that meets their needs and elevates them to a higher moral level.

By providing a vision of what can be achieved by positively motivating others to realize it, by giving clarity and articulation to a company's guiding values, and by setting a personal example of doing the right thing, entrepreneurs can and do mobilize people to do something socially useful that meets their needs, provides benefits to a wider community, and even contributes to elevating others to a higher moral level. Entrepreneurs may not think of outcomes of their company-building activity that way, but from my observation that's exactly what they achieve. This is why entrepreneurship requires a consideration of values and morals—of combining what is done with how it is done.

There's also a very practical reason for a values-based, morally rigorous view of entrepreneurship. That is usually the only viable way for an entrepreneur to do business in the long run.

The Most Valuable Possession

An entrepreneur's most valuable possession in the business world is not money or products or facilities. It's his or her reputation. If one lies, cheats, or steals, then the marketplace usually learns of that and the liar, cheater, and thief loses any credibility that he or she may have had. On the other hand, those who act with integrity and an abundance or sharing mentality, as Steven Covey points out in his book, *Principle Centered Leadership*, enhance their credibility in the marketplace and draw others who want to do business with them.

Arthur Ashe wrote about the importance of reputation to him in his moving memoir, *Days of Grace*:

> *If one's reputation is a possession, then of all my possessions, my reputation means most to me. Nothing even comes close to it in importance. I know that I haven't always lived without error or sin, but I also know that I have tried hard to be honest and good at all times. When I fail, my conscience comes alive. It is crucial to me that people think of me as honest and principled. In turn, to ensure that they do, I must always act in an honest and principled fashion, no matter the cost. I want no stain on my character, no blemish on my reputation.*

The great majority of entrepreneurs think and act very much the same way. They thus not only build more viable and lasting enterprises, but they also live more happily.

The reputations of entrepreneurs are shaped not by what happens to them, but rather by how they respond to what happens to them. This is the lesson of the sweet movie *Groundhog Day*. The protagonist, played by Bill Murray, finds himself trapped in the situation of a constantly repeating day. But he changes from a selfish, egotistical, and manipulative individual into a person of significant accomplishment and credible conduct by taking the initiative to act with integrity and an abundance of sharing mentality. He thus makes himself deserving of honor.

By providing a vision that is personal, positive and larger than oneself, by dealing honestly in negotiations, by creating guidelines for responsible risk-taking, learning, and innovation in their companies, and by building community within and outside their organizations, entrepreneurs can and do develop successful enterprises that also mobilize people to do something that is socially useful. There's honor in that.

47

Sustaining Values

E ntrepreneurship is a values-driven endeavor. The very act of starting and building something of significance should require a consideration of values—of combining what is done with how it is done. But what values may be particularly important in guiding the entrepreneur?

One particularly provocative and enlightening set of values has emerged from the Native American community. Michele Lansdowne, from the Salish and Kootenai tribes in Montana, and Lisa Little Chief Bryan, from the Lakota tribes in South Dakota, have developed an entrepreneurship curriculum that focuses on the questions, choices, and obstacles that entrepreneurs may face when growing their businesses in Indian country. Their list of values and the way they tie these values to business development serve as a guide for each of us.

- *Bravery*. In recognizing and pursuing an opportunity, an entrepreneur requires bravery. Bravery, which springs from a natural creativity and a determined spirit, helps the entrepreneur deal with discouragement and even defeat in the early stages of company formation.
- *Vision*. Vision guides the entrepreneur through the business planning process. Vision, which directs the entrepreneur in clarifying the opportunity and setting goals for the organization, allows the entrepreneur to see past his or her current position and beyond limited resources to more fully appreciate the potential of the venture.
- *Respect for self and others*. Respect for oneself and others is essential for the individual to appreciate his or her efforts, to relate effectively to one's family and community, and to motivate others. This respect, which stems from pride, hope, and enthusiasm, frees the entrepreneur from the obstacles of low self-esteem, hopelessness, and anger.
- *Trust*. Trust is an indispensable part of the marketing effort as the company grows. Trust, which results from reliability, compassion, and gentleness, permits the entrepreneur to overcome mistrust, selfishness, and ruthlessness as the company deals with employees, customers, and vendors.
- *Honesty*. An entrepreneur must have honesty in financing the company and managing the assets of the firm. Honesty, which emanates from decisiveness in taking risk and making choices, lets the entrepreneur avoid false security and stay calm amid confusing situations.

▌ *Generosity.* In directing the management and operations of a growing business, an entrepreneur should be generous. Generosity, which develops from supporting and leading others, permits an entrepreneur to eliminate racial bias, reduce resistance to change, and heal dysfunctions within the organization.

▌ *Fortitude.* An entrepreneur requires fortitude to keep a business strong and eventually bring it to harvest. Fortitude, which stems from persistence, realism, and consistency, strengthens the entrepreneur against scattered thinking and giving up.

Entrepreneurs who are guided by a set of values, like these developed for the Native American entrepreneurship program, enhance their credibility in the marketplace and draw others who want to do business with them. Sometimes entrepreneurs can get so caught up in the new, new thing—the latest, greatest product, service or technology—that they fail to see and appreciate what actually sustains them, their employees, and their enterprises over the long term. By thinking of themselves as brave, visionary, respectful, trustworthy, honest, generous, and fortitudinous, entrepreneurs can maintain a true north direction in their lives and companies.

I like the set of values that emerged from the Native American community. They inspire while they inform. They emphasize that character is critical in the company-building process. They provide a standard and a challenge for any entrepreneur who seeks to build a viable and lasting enterprise. And they remind us that true success—and, I'd contend, a happier life—stems from enlightened values that direct behavior.

48

The Right Question

Can entrepreneurship be taught?

Some people, including many entrepreneurs, say absolutely not. They argue that entrepreneurs are "born." The hidden assumption in this argument is that there is only a small, select number of people who have what it takes to start and build companies. Yet evidence abounds that lots of people from all kinds of backgrounds are launching their own enterprises today.

Once, it was argued that management skills couldn't be taught. A good manager was a "born manager." But today, teaching management is something we take for granted. At one time a similar debate was under way about leadership. Yet today, we help people learn leadership.

I don't think entrepreneurs are born. There isn't a DNA gene stamped with an "E" for entrepreneur in someone's genetic makeup. So something else must be at work in the development of entrepreneurs.

Entrepreneurial drive and ability reside in many people who thus have the potential to become successful entrepreneurs, if they are given the opportunity to learn and extend that drive and ability. Isn't that what education should be about: providing the knowledge, experience, and environment to learn and grow?

Every effective entrepreneur demonstrates "fire in the belly." That's the wellspring of passion, which gives meaning to the venture that an entrepreneur undertakes, and which also sparks the need and desire to learn.

Can Entrepreneurs Learn?

Thus, the question "Can entrepreneurship be taught?" actually is the wrong question. The right question is, "Can entrepreneurs learn?" Every entrepreneur I ask gives me the same response, "Yes, and let me tell you what I want to learn, what I need to learn, what I wish I had learned earlier and faster."

So, if the question is modified, the answer becomes more obvious. Can entrepreneurs learn? Absolutely! In fact, successful entrepreneurs are exceptional learners.

Today, entrepreneurship education is causing a sea change in curriculum, teaching methodologies, and experiential learning at colleges and universities around the country. A recent survey by George Washington University has revealed that more than 1,400 colleges and universities have courses, programs, and centers in entrepreneurship. Why is this happening?

I remember a discussion with the dean of a leading business school who commented that entrepreneurship is a subset of management. "No," I replied, "Management is a subset of entrepreneurship."

Entrepreneurship as a Business Discipline

Entrepreneurship is flourishing at business schools because it is a genuinely integrative discipline. It actually requires somebody to do everything, to apply an integrated set of conceptual and practical skills to starting and building an enterprise. These include skills such as communication, selling, and negotiation.

The abilities to identify and pursue opportunity, to innovate, to marshal resources, and to acquire know-how make entrepreneurship an incredibly dynamic human endeavor. Schools around the country are helping students learn how to do these.

I see two approaches that undergraduate and graduate programs are using to weave entrepreneurship into their curriculums. One strategy is to set up a series of separate undergraduate and graduate courses, programs, and initiatives specifically focused on entrepreneurship. Consequently, for example, we see the emergence of "entrepreneurship concentrations" in MBA schools. A second strategy is to take these entrepreneurial elements and infuse them into a core curriculum that already exists. This requires finding ways to inculcate into traditional marketing, finance, and management courses themes of opportunity recognition, resourcefulness, innovation, and harvesting.

Another way to think about curriculum is to ask ourselves, "What is it that entrepreneurs do, and what do they need to know to do it?" The answer changes the way faculty construct curriculums. This is the core of a "performance-based" curriculum versus the more traditional "subject-based" curriculum. Performance-based focuses on skills and tasks. A subject-based curriculum focuses on knowledge. A performance-based curriculum focuses on what you do, whereas a subject-based curriculum focuses on what you know.

In the competitive marketplace, more and more aspiring entrepreneurs are asking and expecting the schools they attend to provide opportunities for experience-based learning, such as entrepreneurship internships, business plan writing, and actual company startup initiatives.

Today, more and more undergraduate and, especially, graduate students are launching companies directly from the classroom to the marketplace. There are practical reasons for this. They often enter programs with four or five years of business experience, come with the stated intention to own their own ventures, enter programs that are designed to facilitate the startup of a company, and in the course of the program, develop the skills and contacts that contribute to venture success.

I am convinced that entrepreneurship can be taught—that entrepreneurs can learn—and that all students ought to be exposed to the entrepreneurial process to appreciate what an entrepreneur does and how he or she does it. As that happens, higher education will take on a remarkably dynamic, creative, and forward-looking role into the twenty-first century.

49

Kid Entrepreneurs

Not only was I a kid once, I was actually a kid entrepreneur—although I did not know it at the time. You see, when I was a kid, entrepreneurship and education never went together. No one in all my K–12 classroom years ever taught me about entrepreneurship, or encouraged me to consider starting a business as a career alternative, or even told me that as a kid I could run a business. But as I look back, I know now that I did anyway, and that I learned lessons from those first entrepreneurial encounters—lessons about the relationship between work and opportunity, about adding value to what one does and with whom one does it, and about dealing with uncertainty—that serve me well today.

I became an independent businessperson (notice I did not say entrepreneur) when I was nine years old. A district manager for the old *Cleveland News* offered me a paper route when the paperboy who had been delivering the papers moved away. The route was already established in the neighborhood, and my job was simply to maintain it.

I actually became an entrepreneur the following year. I didn't like the fact that the *Cleveland News*, as an afternoon paper, kept interfering with my after-school playtime, so I became proactive in trying to get a paper route with the *Cleveland Plain Dealer*, which was the morning paper. Through persistence, I learned that a new apartment building was just opening up and that the *Plain Dealer* was looking for a boy to deliver papers in the highrise. Even though the apartment at the start had no customers, would necessitate an immediate drop in my income for an unknown period of time, and would mean giving up a sure route that I had mastered, I jumped at the opportunity!

In what seemed like no time at all, I had the proverbial bird's nest on the ground. A single building, protected from the snow and rain, with nearly a hundred customers (all of whom were new and—by signing them up during contests at the paper—allowed me to win not one but two new bikes, one for me and one for my brother). I was soon making more money than I had before while having the time I wanted to play in the afternoon. That was entrepreneurial!

Entrepreneurial Encounters of the First Kind

A lot of today's entrepreneurs were kid entrepreneurs also—maybe they had a paper route, or a babysitting service, or a lawn-mowing or snow-shoveling operation, or even a lemonade stand.

These entrepreneurial encounters of the first kind can be life affecting because they are personal, positive, and emotional.

Think of the great paradigm shift for education that kid entrepreneurs represent. By pursuing opportunity, creating value, and tolerating ambiguity, they show the power and ability that kids have to start and run businesses, to force education into a far more contextual, experiential, hands-on learning mode, and to move from concrete to general principles rather than vice versa.

We need to nurture and develop more kid entrepreneurs, just as we need to nurture and develop scientists, professionals, and artists. I would contend that entrepreneurship education provides an unparalleled opportunity to develop skills, principles, attitudes, and behaviors that not only can help prepare one for life's journey, but also help guide one through it. This is because entrepreneurship is such an intensely human process. It involves turning dreams into realities and dealing with the consequences of both failure and success. It requires working with and through other people, and having the confidence and ability to try new things, to overcome obstacles, and to strive for a goal that's larger than oneself.

We need to make entrepreneurship part of our educational process. This requires, as Marilyn Kourilsky at the Kauffman Center for Entrepreneurial Leadership emphasizes, a paradigm shift: "Don't take a job. Make a job."

Does this mean that all kids should be entrepreneurs? No. Just as all kids cannot and should not be scientists (though we expect them to learn science), or writers (though we expect them to appreciate literature), or engineers (though we want them to know mathematics). But should kids have the opportunity to be exposed to the entrepreneurial process, to experience firsthand the problem-solving and critical-thinking skills required to launch and build a company, and to understand and appreciate the workings of an economic system that make entrepreneurial choices possible? I am certain the answer is yes! Entrepreneurship, by combining thinking and doing, can help develop young men and women of intelligent and responsible action.

Instilling Trust

We sense that our current educational system isn't working (at least not very well). Ernest Boyer, the late president of the Carnegie Foundation for Education, in his book, *Ready to Learn*, described eight major themes that he argued are essential for education reform. One of these is the theme of producing/consuming.

Kids know all about consuming. In the movie *Postcards from the Edge*, Shirley McClain accuses her daughter, Meryl Streep, of seeking instant gratification, to which she replies, "That's too long!" We need to teach kids about producing—about the relationship between work and consumption, about the process of and requirements for creating value, and about the benefits of delayed gratification.

A report compiled for the Kauffman Foundation on the school-to-work transition found a disheartening consensus among studies and commissions that concluded that the United States has the worst school-to-work transition of any advanced industrial economy in the world. Education in America today, the report summarized, is rarely connected to training or jobs; youth flounder in the labor market; and as a result, we face unemployment, poverty, and dislocation among far too many of our youth. The area of entrepreneurship is a glaring gap in curriculums.

We know from extensive research that kids live up or down to our expectations. What we see in them helps shape what they see in themselves. If we expect kids to be able to start companies, if we genuinely believe that they can create and run enterprises, then we reinforce their belief in the future and in the possibilities of things.

If not, we can anticipate the result. The great American poet Langston Hughes warned us what can happen when we lose our belief in the future: "What happens to a dream deferred? Does it dry up like a raisin in the sun, or does it explode?"

My son Matthew in one of his earlier ventures as a kid entrepreneur, developed a marketing flier to launch a babysitting service. I was struck by his motto: "Finally someone you trust." On first reading, I knew that he wanted to communicate the key benefit that all parents want as they walk out the door and leave their child in the care of someone else. But after thinking about it further, it had an additional meaning for me.

"Finally someone you trust" should also apply to oneself.

Perhaps this should be the goal of all of our efforts in entrepreneurship education—of every program, initiative, and curriculum, of each project, course, and technology—to have each and every boy and girl, at the completion of it, say to himself or herself, "Finally someone you trust," and mean themselves. If we do that, we will surely have helped prepare them for whatever life may bring.

50

PROFILE:
Genius at Work

He takes with him wherever he goes a story, a box of slides, and a contagious passion. His story tells the tale of a potter turned entrepreneur. His box of slides reveals the transforming power of art and education. His passion instigates social change.

Bill Strickland grew up in the Manchester community of Pittsburgh as it deteriorated from a healthy community to a ghetto, as many inner cities in America did in the 1950s and 1960s. While in high school, he became fascinated with pottery and fell in love with the ceramic arts. Working at the potter's wheel released his creativity. Becoming a ceramic artist spurred his desire for learning. He went on to graduate from the University of Pittsburgh.

While still in college, he started the Manchester Craftsman's Guild in 1968 as an after-school program "to educate and inspire inner city youth to become productive citizens." His vision was to use art to change the lives of at-risk youth, as he had been. "The message here is one of hope. That's what the arts are about. Hope." So out of a small space in his old neighborhood, he taught kids how to mold clay and in the process how to mold their own lives.

Three years later, he was asked to take over the Bidwell Training Center, which had been launched by the Presbyterian Church in response to the riots of 1968 to provide vocational training to economically disadvantaged individuals. The Center had encountered problems with the Internal Revenue Service for failing to pay withholding taxes. It was forced to shut down or find someone to rebuild it. Where others saw a disaster, Bill saw an opportunity for a remarkable and unique combination of forces. To him the arts provided an accessible, cost-effective way to instill creative thinking while vocational training brought enthusiasm and meaning to tasks. What better way to tap the potential of individuals!

"I've got some pictures I want to show you," he will tell audiences at business schools and conferences and even Senate hearings. There on the screen are snapshots of beautiful ceramic pieces, compelling photographs, and culinary creations by the students in his programs. There are frames of lofty arched hallways, lovely large flowerpots along spotless corridors, spacious classrooms, elaborately equipped laboratories, and an impressive performing arts auditorium where the people in his programs come to learn. And there are faces—of chefs in white hats, of technicians in starched coats, of musicians on stage, and of young artists at work.

Bill Strickland knows what it took to make each and every slide a reality. He explains how to change people's senses of reality.

He looks for a positive attitude and a willingness to learn. He talks about insisting on excellence, creating an environment of beauty, raising expectations, and building self-esteem.

Through the constant recognition and pursuit of opportunity, he built both the Guild and the Center. He won over foundations and corporations to help fund his vision. He added photography, music, and the visual arts to his programs. He expanded his vocational training curriculums. He started a culinary school.

By the early 1980s, he needed more space, better equipment, and modern laboratories. So he decided to build a new, world-class facility to house his growing enterprise. He raised $9 million and constructed a state-of-the-art, 62,000-square-foot facility in his neighborhood in 1986. His one key requirement—it had to be beautiful. Even though the building is in an area of warehouses, factories, and urban blight, there is no graffiti or drugs or crime here. Instead, hope, expectation, and results. Most young people go on to college; most adults find fulfilling work.

To meet community needs, he expanded the Bidwell Training Center to include information sciences, pharmacy, medical transcription, and medical claims processing. He started a business incubator for women and minority entrepreneurs. He got Bayer Corporation to fund the development and teaching of a curriculum to train chemical lab technicians and then to place them in their laboratories. His culinary school gained so much acclaim that people started to request catering service. So he set up the for-profit Bidwell Food Services, which now operates a 200-seat restaurant and provides services for clients like the Pittsburgh International Airport. Its after-tax profits support the programs of the Guild and the Center.

Because he loves jazz, he set up a state-of-the-art-recording studio with his auditorium, and recruited renowned jazz artists to give performances. On a visit to Bayer, he found out that the company is a leading producer of polycarbonate, the plastic from which CDs are made. He had the music and Bayer had the CDs, so he struck a deal that included Sony to produce five recordings with the proceeds from the first 25,000 units going to the Manchester Craftsmen's Guild. His first CD with the Count Basie Orchestra with the New York Voices won a Grammy award for best performance by a large jazz ensemble.

Bill has learned that nonprofits are businesses, not just causes, and that nonprofit does not mean nonrevenue generating! One of his latest projects is the Denali Initiative, a program to train leaders in the nonprofit sector to become more entrepreneurial in their efforts to meet community needs.

Among his awards, recognitions, and special appointments, Bill was presented with a MacArthur Fellowship Grant, the "genius" award, in 1996 for his leadership and ingenuity in the arts. Part of his genius has been in showing a new model of social enterprise, of applying entrepreneurial skills to some of our most perplexing social problems, and of demonstrating the "art" of entrepreneurship in community development.

Potter, educator, and social entrepreneur, Bill Strickland is still writing his own story. And he is still willing to talk about his box of slides to anyone who will listen.

EPILOGUE:
The Entrepreneur's Virtue

Some of the entrepreneurs featured in this book will not succeed. Some of the ventures will not survive. Despite genuine passion, excellent business plans, and well-financed ventures, some founders and firms will fail. The passion of some will not overcome poor timing or unresponsive customers. The unexpected and unforeseen will foil some of the best-laid plans. Money alone will not solve the technological problems of some products and services.

All the entrepreneurs featured in this book will face other challengers. All the ventures will encounter rivals. New contenders will vie for share of mind as well as share of market. Existing competitors will introduce improved products and provide better services. The entrepreneurs and companies discussed in this book, like all the others in the marketplace, will be pushed to find creative solutions to problems, to rapidly take advantage of opportunities, to compete.

This is as it should be. This is how the entrepreneurial process works. An entrepreneurial economy requires a constant stream of innovation to stay responsive and vital and growing. It requires a continual source of innovators; of dreamers who do; of visionaries who creatively destroy the status quo and in the process build new industries, generate jobs, create wealth, and contribute to economic and social well-being. It requires entrepreneurs.

Theodore Roosevelt pointed out that the credit belongs to the person "who does actually strive to do the deeds; who knows the great enthusiasm, the great devotions; who spends himself in a worthy cause; who at the best knows in the end the triumph of high achievement, and who at the worst, if he fails, at least fails while daring greatly, so that his place shall never be with those cold and timid souls who knew neither victory nor defeat." Whether in victory or defeat, entrepreneurs deserve credit for striving to actually start and build enterprises, and for facing head-on the challenges that come with that endeavor.

Those who make it and those who don't share an internal source of renewal that makes them willing to risk failure to try to achieve success. They share the abiding virtue of entrepreneurs: hope. I've become convinced that hope is the best virtue of entrepreneurs. Every company will face obstacles, disappointments, and crises. The ones that survive and thrive will have leaders who are purveyors of hope. The Talmud teaches that on Judgment Day the first question we will face is, "Did you live with hope?" I like the thought of this question.

Hope gives credence to dreams. In his wonderful travelogue of his trek across America, *Blue Highways*, William Least Heat-Moon comes across a boat builder who is building a very large boat next to a very tiny stream. Moon asks him why he is doing this. The boat builder says that it's been his dream to build this boat and he needs the space. Moon then asks if dreams take up a lot of space. "All you'll give them," the boat builder replies.

Every entrepreneur, as well as every investor who bets on the entrepreneur, has to live with hope. With hope, all things are possible, even the impossible. With hope comes the belief that one can make things happen, that a person can have influence over his or her environment, that people can change, and companies can develop. With hope, optimism is possible; the glass is always half full, even when it's pretty much empty. We need this kind of hope in our economy and our society.

The possibilities that hope can engender were powerfully captured in the closing scene of the film *The Shawshank Redemption*. Red, played by Morgan Freeman, is released from Shawshank prison after spending nearly his entire life behind its walls. He begins to feel desperate in his inability to adjust to the outside world. Then he finds a box, which includes money and a note, left for him by his friend, Andy, played by Tim Robbins, who had escaped from Shawshank through a daring plan. Andy tells Red in the note: "Hope is a good thing, maybe the best of things, and no good thing ever dies." Red sets out to find Andy in Mexico and start a new life. He is transformed with the possibilities ahead of him: "I'm so excited I can barely sit still or hold a thought in my head. I hope that I can make it across the border. I hope to see my friend and shake his hand. I hope the Pacific is as blue as it has been in my dreams. I hope."

John Gardner in his excellent book *Self-Renewal* stresses the role of "tough-minded optimism" in people who create lives full of meaning, purpose, and achievement. "Both the tough-mindedness and the optimism are immensely important. High hopes that are dashed by the first failure are precisely what we don't need. We need to believe in ourselves but not to believe that life is easy. Nothing in the historical record tells us that triumph is assured."

The entrepreneurs in this book believe in themselves; they know that company building is not easy. And so, even those who may not make it are just as much role models for the rest of us as those who do because they can teach us about combining guts and logic, about the power of hope, even in the most difficult of circumstances, and about daring greatly.

Endnotes

Introduction

See Malcolm Gladwell, *The Tipping Point: How Little Things Can Make a Big Difference* (Little, Brown and Company: Boston, 2000).

Data on aspiring entrepreneurs comes from Paul D. Reynolds, Michael Hay, and S. Michael Camp, *Global Entrepreneurship Monitor* report (Kauffman Center for Entrepreneurial Leadership, 1999); annual surveys conducted by the Gallup organization (see, for example, *Youth and Entrepreneurship: A Report from A Gallup Survey*, Kauffman Center for Entrepreneurial Leadership, 1996); George Solomon, "The National Survey of Entrepreneurial Education, 1997–1998," George Washington University, 1998; and program data on youth entrepreneurship by the Kauffman Center for Entrepreneurial Leadership. Data on lifestyle entrepreneurs comes from Small Business Administration data on incorporations and on minority businesses; "SOHO: The New Summit on the Business Horizon," prepared and published by Working Solo, Inc., 1999; K. Cheney, "You Can Make Six Figures Working at Home," *Money*, March 1996, pp. 74–87; and reports from the National Foundation for Women Business Owners. Data on growth entrepreneurs comes from studies by David Birch at Cognetics, Inc.; information from entrepreneur associations; and evaluations by the Kauffman Center for Entrepreneurial Leadership.

Chapter 1

For further information on the entrepreneurs featured here, see *Entrepreneur Of The Year* magazine, published by Ernst & Young, LLP, fall 1999.

Chapter 2

See Lee Bolman and Terry Deal, *Leading with Soul: An Uncommon Journey* (San Francisco: Jossey-Bass Publishers, 1995); and John Ketteringham and P. Ranganath Nayak, *Breakthroughs!* (New York: Rawson Associates, 1986).

Chapter 3

For further information on the study of leadership skills of entrepreneurs conducted by the Center for Creative Leadership, see John Eggers and Raymond Smilor, "Leadership Skill of Entrepreneurs; Resolving the Paradoxes and Enhancing the Practices of Entrepreneurial Growth" in Raymond Smilor and Donald Sexton, editors, *Leadership and Entrepreneurship* (Westport, CT: Quorum Books, 1996). See Jack Stack, *The Great Game of Business* (New York: Double Day, 1992); and Margaret Wheatley, *Leadership and the New Science* (San Francisco: Barett-Kohler Publishing Co., 1993). Timothy Hoeksema is featured in *Entrepreneur Of The Year* magazine, published by Ernst & Young, LLP, fall 1999.

Chapter 4

The quote from Jim Collins comes from his article, "What Comes Next," *Inc.*, October 1997, pp. 40–49. The quote from Rick Krska comes from a video on entrepreneurship developed by the Kauffman Center for Entrepreneurial Leadership.

Chapter 5

On optimism, see Martin E. P. Seligman, *Learned Optimism* (New York: Alfred. A. Knopf, 1991). Jonathan Coon's quote comes from his 2000 application for the Entrepreneur Of The Year program.

Chapter 7

For more information on Three Dog Bakery, see Dan Dye and Mark Beckloff, *Short Tails and Treats from Three Dog Bakery* (Kansas City, MO: Andrews and McMeel, 1996), and *The Entrepreneurial Revolution*, a documentary film on entrepreneurship presented by the Public Broadcasting Service (1996).

Chapter 8

For more on the Harvard Business School definition of entrepreneurship, see Howard Stevenson and David Gumpert, "The Heart of Entrepreneurship," *Harvard Business Review* 63 (March–April): 85–94. On bisociation, see Arthur Koestler, *The Act of Creation*, (New York:

Viking, 1990). For further information on the entrepreneurs featured here, see *Entrepreneur Of The Year* magazine, published by Ernst & Young, LLP, fall 1998 and fall 1999.

Chapter 9

See Norman MacLean, *Young Men and Fire* (Chicago: University of Chicago Press, 1992); and Stephen R. Covey, *The 7 Habits of Highly Effective People* (New York: Simon & Schuster, 1989). For further information on the entrepreneurs featured here, see the *Entrepreneur Of The Year* magazine, published by Ernst & Young, LLP, fall 1998 and fall 1999.

Chapter 10

The Jennifer Lawton quote comes from her comments during the Kauffman Center for Entrepreneurial Leadership's Thought Leaders Session (May 1999). See William B. Walstad and Marilyn L. Kourilsky, *Seeds of Success: Entrepreneurship and Youth*, (Kansas City, MO: Kauffman Center for Entrepreneurial Leadership, 1999).

Chapter 11

For further information on the entrepreneurs featured here, see the *Entrepreneur Of The Year* magazine, published by Ernst & Young, LLP, fall 1998 and fall 1999.

Chapter 12

See Regis McKenna, *The Regis Touch: Million-Dollar Advice from America's Top Marketing Consultant* (Reading, MA: Addison-Wesley, 1985).

Chapter 13

See Marilyn Kourilsky, "Entrepreneurship Education: Opportunity in Search of Curriculum," a paper published by the Kauffman Center for Entrepreneurial Leadership, 1995; Peter Drucker, "Not Enough Generals Were Killed," in Frances Hesselbein, Marshall Goldsmith, and Richard Beckhard, editors, *Leader of the Future* (San Francisco: Jossey-Bass Publishers, 1996). The quote from Kay Hammer comes from "Inner Strength," *Entrepreneur*, August 1998, p. 77.

Chapter 15

For a complete biography on Ewing Kauffman, see Anne Morgan, *Prescription for Success: The Life and Values of Ewing Marion Kauffman* (Kansas City, MO: Andrews and McMeel, 1995).

Chapter 16

For more on networks and entrepreneurship, see Howard Aldrich and Catherine Zimmer, "Entrepreneurship Through Social Networks," in Donald Sexton and Raymond Smilor, editors, *The Art and Science of Entrepreneurship* (Cambridge, MA: Ballinger Publishing Co., 1986), pp. 3–23.

Chapter 17

Ken Meyers and Jim McCann are featured in a video on selling for entrepreneurs, *Successful Selling for Entrepreneurs: Helping Customers Buy* (Kauffman Center for Entrepreneurial Leadership, 1995).

Chapter 19

See Everett Rogers, *The Diffusion of Innovation* (New York: The Free Press, 1995).

Chapter 20

The example of Tom Velez comes from Mabel Tinjaca's *Vision! Hispanic Entrepreneurs in the United States*, (Pleasant Hill, Missouri: Heritage Publishing Company, 2001). Scott Cook is featured in the PBS show, *The Entrepreneurial Revolution*. See Warren Bennis and Patricia Ward Biederman, *Organizing Genius: The Secrets of Creative Collaboration*, (Reading, MA: Addison-Wesley, 1997).

Chapter 21

Pat Cloherty and Cathy Hughes are featured on the audiotape, *Women Entrepreneurs: Launching and Leading Successful Ventures*, produced by the Kauffman Center for Entrepreneurial Leadership (1998). Jack Stack is featured on the PBS show, *The Entrepreneurial Revolution*. The quote from Jim Collins comes from his article, "The Learning Executive," *Inc.*, August 1997, pp. 35–36.

Chapter 22

The quote from Jim McCann comes from a video on selling for entrepreneurs, *Successful Selling for Entrepreneurs: Helping Customers Buy* (Kauffman Center for Entrepreneurial Leadership, 1995).

Chapter 23

For data on business plans, see Donald Sexton and Forrest Seal, *Leading Practices of Fast Growth Entrepreneurs: Pathways for High Performance* (Kansas City, MO: National Center for Entrepreneurship Research at the Kauffman Center for Entrepreneurial Leadership, 1997).

Chapter 27

See Sun Tzu, *The Art of War* (New York: Random House, 1988); Joseph Schumpeter, *The Theory of Economic Development* (Cambridge, MA: Harvard University Press, 1934); Peter Drucker, *Innovation and Entrepreneurship: Practice and Principles* (New York: HarperBusiness, 1985); Herbert A. Simon, "What We Know About the Creative Process," in Robert Lawrence Kuhn, editor, *Frontiers in Creative and Innovative Management* (Cambridge, MA: Ballinger Publishing Co., 1985). Pierre Omidyar is featured in *Entrepreneur Of The Year* magazine, published by Ernst & Young, LLP, fall 1999.

Chapter 28

See Jim Taylor and Watts Wacker, *The 500 Year Delta: What Comes After What Comes Next* (New York: HarperBusiness, 1997); and Shona L. Brown and Kathleen M. Eisenhardt, *Competing on the Edge: Strategy as Structured Chaos* (Boston: Harvard Business School Press, 1998). Bill Harris is featured in the PBS show, *The Entrepreneurial Revolution*.

Chapter 29

Dick Schulze is featured in *Entrepreneur Of The Year* magazine, published by Ernst & Young, LLP, fall 1999.

Chapter 30

See *The Fool Rules!*, The Motley Fool, Inc., 1997.

Chapter 32

Scott Cook is featured in the PBS show, *The Entrepreneurial Revolution.* The quote from Michael Moritz comes from Michael S. Malone, "What's Next? Hot Markets of the Future," *Upside.com* (June 4, 1997), p. 14.

Chapter 33

The Andy Sack quotes come from his article, "Angel Financing: Dos and Don'ts for Entrepreneurs," which appeared on the Kauffman Center for Entrepreneurial Leadership Web site, *entreworld.org* (December 1998).

Chapter 36

The Audrey MacLean quote comes from Mary Beth Grover, "Starting a company is like going to war," *Forbes*, November 2, 1998.

Chapter 37

The quotes from Jeff and Millie Thomas come from the PBS show, *The Entrepreneurial Revolution*, in which they were featured. Penny McConnell's story was featured on page 8B in *USA Today*, May 26, 1999. Bill Passman's experience was reported by Chris Arnold in a story on "Failure in Silicon Valley" on National Public Radio, February 12, 1997. The data on bankruptcies, failures, and terminations was compiled by the U.S. Small Business Administration, Office of Advocacy.

Chapter 38

See Richard Osborne, "Entrepreneurial Renewal," *Business Horizons*, November–December 1992, pp. 58–63.

Chapter 40

Doug Kahn provided his perspective on what entrepreneurs could expect at a training module of the Kauffman Fellows Program (Austin, TX, April 1995).

Chapter 42

See Max Carey, *The Superman Complex: Achieving the Balance that Leads to Success* (Atlanta: Longstreet, Inc., 1999).

Chapter 43
Steve Lazarus provided his perspective on the role of directors at a training module of the Kauffman Fellows Program (Berkeley, CA, April 1999).

Chapter 44
See John C. Weicher, "The Rich and the Poor: Demographics of the U.S. Wealth Distribution," *Federal Reserve Bank of St. Louis Review*, v. 79, n. 4 July–August 1997, pp. 25–37; Michael Stolper, *Wealth: An Owner's Manual* (New York: HarperBusiness, 1993); Doug Levy, "Net elite: 'It's not about money'," *USA Today*, February 22, 1999, p. 1B; Carolyn T. Geer, "Turning employees into stakeholders," *Forbes*, December 1, 1997, pp. 154–160.

Chapter 45
See John Gardner, "Building Community" (Washington, DC: Independent Sector, 1991). Roberto Alfaro is featured in the PBS show, *The Entrepreneurial Revolution*.

Chapter 46
See Ronald A. Heifetz, *Leadership Without Easy Answers* (Cambridge, MA: The Belknap Press of the Harvard University Press, 1994); Stephen R. Covey, *Principle-Centered Leadership* (New York: Simon & Schuster, 1992); Arthur Ashe, *Days of Grace: A Memoir* (New York: Alfred A. Knopf, 1993).

Chapter 47
See Michele Lansdowne, *American Indian Entrepreneurs: Flathead Reservation Case Studies* (Pablo, Montana: Salish Kootenai College Press, 1999), and Lisa Little Chief Bryan, *American Indian Entrepreneurs: Rosebud and Pine Ridge Reservations Case Studies* (Pablo, Montana: Salish Kootenai College Press, 1999).

Chapter 48
George Solomon, "The National Survey of Entrepreneurship Education, 1997–1998," George Washington University, 1998.

Chapter 49

See Ernest Boyer, *Ready to Learn: A Mandate for the Nation*, Carnegie Foundation for the Advancement of Teaching, (Lawrenceville, NJ: Princeton University Press, 1991); and "Reweaving The Tattered Web: Socializing and Enculturing Our Children About School-To-Work Transition" (Kansas City, MO: Ewing Marion Kauffman Foundation, 1993).

Chapter 50

The quote from Bill Strickland comes from Gil Ott, "Art in Context: Industrial Pittsburgh Catching Up With Bill Strickland," *High Performance*, 67, fall 1994. For further information, see the case "Bidwell Training Center, Inc., and Manchester Craftsmen's Guild: Preparation in Pittsburgh" (Boston: Publishing Division, Harvard Business School, 1993).

Epilogue

See William Least Heat-Moon, *Blue Highways: A Journey into America* (Boston: Little, Brown and Company, 1982); John Gardner, *Self-Renewal: The Individual and the Innovative Society* (New York: Harper & Rowe, 1964).

Kauffman Center for Entrepreneurial Leadership at the Ewing Marion Kauffman Foundation

Ewing Marion Kauffman established the Ewing Marion Kauffman Foundation to pursue a vision of self-sufficient people in healthy communities. The Foundation, with an endowment of more than $2 billion, is based in Kansas City, Missouri. It directs and supports innovative programs and initiatives that merge the social and economic dimensions of philanthropy locally and nationally.

The Foundation's mission is to research and identify the unfulfilled needs of society and to develop, implement, or fund breakthrough solutions that have a lasting impact and give people a choice and hope for the future. In pursuit of its vision and mission, the Kauffman Foundation works to help youth become productive members of society and to accelerate entrepreneurship in America.

The Kauffman Center for Entrepreneurial Leadership is taking an innovative approach to accelerating entrepreneurship through educational programming and research. Inspired by his passion to provide opportunity for other entrepreneurs, Ewing Marion Kauffman launched the Kauffman Center, the largest organization solely focused on entrepreneurial success at all levels—from elementary students to high-growth entrepreneurs.

The Center's entrepreneurial activities are organized around three primary areas. It develops and disseminates innovative, effective, and comprehensive curricula and support systems for adult entrepreneurs, from aspiring to high growth. Its youth entrepreneurship efforts focus on creative initiatives for enhancing entrepreneurship awareness, readiness, and application experiences for K–12 youth and community college students. It also promotes entrepreneurship with public policy makers, not-for-profit leaders, and in urban and rural communities of need.

For more information, visit the Center's Web site at *www.entreworld.org.*

Raymond W. Smilor

As an author, public speaker, investor, consultant, and teacher, Dr. Ray Smilor is a nationally recognized expert in entrepreneurship. He is president of the Foundation for Enterprise Development with offices in LaJolla, California, and Washington, D.C. He was vice president of the Kauffman Center for Entrepreneurial Leadership at the Ewing Marion Kauffman Foundation in Kansas City, Missouri from its startup in 1992 through 2000.

He made the entrepreneurial leap to the Kauffman Center from The University of Texas at Austin, where he earned his Ph.D. in U.S. History. At UT, he became a professor in the Graduate School of Business and served for seven years as executive director of the university's internationally recognized think-tank, the IC^2 Institute.

Ray has published extensively. Among his thirteen books are the co-edited *Entrepreneurship 2000* and *Leadership and Entrepreneurship*. His writings range from referred articles in academic journals to opinion pieces in popular magazines and trade publications.

He is a sought-after motivational speaker, lectures internationally, and provides regular commentaries on the nationally syndicated radio show *Entrepreneurs: Living the American Dream*. He was selected as an Entrepreneur Of The Year in 1990 for his activities in support of entrepreneurship and inducted into the Entrepreneur Of The Year Institute.

Ray's entrepreneurial partner in life is his wife of over thirty years, Judy. For Ray, the start of their relationship was love at first sight. For Judy, it took a couple of years of convincing and a ton of flowers! Together, they have traveled the world, met remarkable people, and shared in the adventure of raising (and being raised by) two great sons, Kevin (18) and Matthew (21).